WHAT THE HELL IS WRONG WITH YOU!?

FOOTNOTES OF A BURNT OUT, PISSED OFF, TEN-YEAR RESTAURANT WORKER

BY: FREDDY GIORDANO

WHAT THE HELL IS WRONG WITH YOU!?

What The Hell Is Wrong With You!?
By: Freddy Giordano

©2001 Tempe Thunder Press
P.O. Box 1791
Tempe, Arizona 85280-1791
www.TempeThunderPress.com

All rights reserved. No part of this book may be reproduced or transmitted in any form, electronic or mechanical, including photocopying, recording, or by any information storage/retrieval system whatsoever!! So there!!

ISBN 0-9720033-0-4
Library of Congress Catalog Number: 200209142 6
Co-publisher – Jeff Strada
Photography – James Mackey and Freddy Giordano
Graphic Design – Freddy Giordano and
    Bridget M. Trosclair (Necatargraphics@AOL.com)
Editing – Kim Rice and Melanie Schmucker
Illustrations – Freddy Giordano
Manufactured by – AZLitho, Tucson, Arizona
Printed in the United States of America!!
Special Thanks to Addam Leveille at Bar Louie, Tempe, Arizona
Photo Cover Acknowledgement:
Special Thanks to:
The Bash On Ash and McDuffy's Sports Bar
230 West Fifth Street, Tempe, Arizona
Roger Egan and Scott Adams, owners
Photo participants from left to right:
Dave Dahlmeier, Freddy Giordano, Travis Tomlin, Kim Ravioli, Nicole Ruscetta, Kevin (KevDog) Smith, Tony Maggio, Jeff Strada

WHAT THE HELL IS WRONG WITH YOU!?

DEDICATED

The most beautiful person who ever lived
Melisa Jean Foster 1972 – 1995

God

All of my friends and family

The quote I live by:
"He who shall, so shall he who."
- *Anonymous* - *Old Norwegian Proverb*

What The Hell Is Wrong With You!?

Foreword

I hate to say it, but this entire idea began as a joke. I wrote out a few stories to share with some friends at the bar that I frequent. People in Tempe, Arizona know the bar as Old Chicago. I worked with the people there. When I did work there, I had never voiced my opinions, but I had them. I believe it was my employment as a bartender at Sky Harbor International Airport that finally opened the bottled up frustration that I've contained within for the past ten years. This is where most of the stories you are about to read come from.

Please keep in mind that this book was written by some schmuck bartender out there with a chip on his shoulder. Some people say that it shows. If it's any consolation, it took quite a bit of time and alcohol to create what you hold in your hands now. I'm okay with that. Like I said, this whole thing started with a joke. I'm not after a Pulitzer here, you know?

I believe that my book gives a realistic account of working in the restaurant industry. I couldn't cover every aspect, of course; therefore I will come out with a second book.

If you have any comments (hopefully good ones!), visit http://www.whatthehelliswrongwithyou.com.

So grab a beer, get comfy, and enjoy the reading. Thanks!

WHAT THE HELL IS WRONG WITH YOU!?

TABLE OF CONTENTS

WHAT THE HELL IS WRONG WITH YOU!?

WHAT THE HELL IS WRONG WITH YOU!?

WHAT THE HELL IS WRONG WITH YOU!?

What The Hell Is Wrong With You!?

Basic Don'ts When You Are Out At The Bar

WHAT THE HELL IS WRONG WITH YOU!?

WHAT THE HELL IS WRONG WITH YOU!?

INTRODUCTION

As we all know, none of us are perfect. I learned this at a very young age. Please take the time to read through this introduction to better understand why I wrote this book.

When I began collecting notes four months ago; I targeted my project towards servers, bartenders, and other restaurant employees that can understand, sympathize and find humor in most of what I would write down. Then I had an epiphany. This could be beneficial to better mankind and rid people of their poorly judged idiosyncrasies and bad habits when visiting a bar or restaurant. Through this, we can lower the anger level of the hospitality industry. In turn, lowering the anger level of the common public. Then who knows, no more gangs, crime goes down, an end to world hunger? Okay, maybe not.

I offer a suggestion to every server, bartender, and hell, even managers to keep this book around at your place of employment. Use it as a quick reference guide. If a customer does something that is in this book, you can pull it out and let them read a funny story. If they say, 'hey, good story', then they didn't get your point, move on. If their brain synapses do seem to all go in the right direction, and they <u>do</u> understand; chances are, they will become a better customer in the future. Once again, further bettering mankind. All in all, you too, can be a controller of fate!

I wrote this book depicting the ongoing struggles between idiots and employees in the restaurant industry. I haven't been the only one to think of this idea. Most people, in and out of the hospitality industry, can and will agree that there resides an unhealthy amount of idiots per capita in any given area. To prove my point, take a good look the next time you see a commercial on television advertising a sports car driving on a lake, or driving on people, or performing any sort of *Dukes of Hazard* style of driving; There will always be fine print at the bottom of the screen saying, 'do not attempt: Professional driver on a closed course'.

WHAT THE HELL IS WRONG WITH YOU!?

Another example: I recently saw a commercial where someone lifted up a vending machine to shake out the product. Again, 'do not attempt'. Duh!

Just take a look at the eye level sticker at every gas pump in the world that says, 'No Smoking'. It hurts me to think that society needs these warnings. It hurts me more to think that some people have probably encountered their demise doing one of these idiotic things. I could just imagine someone pumping gas with a cigarette hanging out of his or her mouth moments before the fireball consumed them. Or imagine someone getting crushed by a vending machine just because they saw it done on TV. All of these things have probably happened at one time or another, and so we need these legal disclaimers. Boggles my mind. This is my premise.

* * *

Seeing that this book is about making fun of the stupid things that other people do, I figured I would first tell you about myself. I have done stupid things as well, just not everyday and I'm not a complete asshole – you'll see what I mean throughout the book. So not to waste any time, let me get started by saying:

"Hi there! Welcome to 'so-and-so' bar and grill! My name is Freddy, how may I assist you?" (Okay, who really talks like that!?)

I'm currently a 26-year-old bartender at a bar in Phoenix Sky Harbor Airport in the beautifully hot valley of the sun. I hear that I'm a really 'nice' guy which, I guess, for the most part, is pretty true; that is until I get pissed off. I'm a Scorpio, I enjoy the outdoors, playing guitar, long romantic walks down the beach...wait a minute, wrong story, sorry.

Believe it or not, I'm a tall, skinny, redheaded Italian kid. You wouldn't believe it if you just met me, but it's true. I'm sure I have a wee touch of the Irish in me. It would explain my no-fused temper and my uncontrollable desire for booze and beer.

WHAT THE HELL IS WRONG WITH YOU!?

Psychologically speaking, I would say that I'm just as screwed up as everyone else. Well, there are a few exceptions to 'everyone else', but they're no fun. Both of my parents have been married and remarried numerous times, making me a 'redheaded stepchild' about seven times over. My family is so dysfunctional, we spell it with an 'i' (get it?). Don't get me wrong out there, I love my family very much, and Trina, if you read this, I love you sis! Please give me a call if you ever have the chance, okay? We all miss you! Case in point.

* * *

The hospitality industry has its good and bad sides for me. Some of the bad things: The stress is horrendous. At times you are expected to do 38 things all at the same time. And in the midst of those 38 things, two or three more people will try to add two or three more things to that list. That's the time when you just have to back up, take a breath to avoid hyperventilating so you can jump back into it again. Believe me, I know.

The conflicts that I have with my stressors usually happen at my place of employment when I reach that 'breaking point'. My anger is one of the hardest things that I have had to deal with. I can't take it out on my friends that I work with, so I take it out on the closest customer. I know that's not the best thing to do, but like the cover says, I'm burnt out and pissed off! Most of the people that I have worked with, and still work with, think it's the funniest thing when I get upset. This usually just makes me angrier, up until we recap the shift with a couple beers. I do feel singled out because when I do get angry, unlike some people that will just crack and cry under the pressure; I blow up and become amusing.

I really don't find it fair. When I see other people getting mad, management or other employees console them. However, when I get pissed off, my managers and coworkers usually make fun of my reactions. At times, I'm just trying to get some people to do the job to make the customer happy. In reality, if the customer's not happy, then I don't get paid! I remember a time at the place at the airport where I work now. It's a perfect example:

* * *

So you know, like many kitchens out there, they 'need a ticket' to make any food. Okay, this is a good thing. Being a manager before, I can completely understand the logistics behind the savings in food cost, and what have you, and yakity-schmackity. I believe that there should be, at times, some exceptions to the 'no ticket' rule. Especially when you keep in consideration these few added aspects: First, We are dealing with fast food, which has a considerably lower food cost ratio. Second, the manager has pulled a Houdini and can't be found. And third, four people are yelling at you because it's taken about 30 minutes for them to get chips and salsa and a damn burrito!

After this table griped at me about how long everything was taking, I first apologized to the table and tried to find out what had happened. I found out that another server took out my food by accident. It happens. Fix the problem. Move on. I brought the other server to the pass through window to the kitchen. I tried to authenticate the fact that I'm neither 'just asking' nor trying to steal food. The cooks told me 'NO', because they, guess what, didn't have a ticket in front of them. I started to get a little upset. I told them the entire situation. At this point, they were finding it all pretty funny. My face was as red as an albino kid that just took a hike through the Sahara. Throughout my pleading, the cooks still gave me the same line, but this time they were laughing about it. Realizing that I'm not going to get the damn sacred burrito, I tried to remain civilized, and searched for a manager. Like any other time at the airport bar, I'd have better luck bench pressing a school bus then finding a manager when I needed one. There like cops. (Just a little side note here. In case one of you big wig corporate people from this very company, we will call 'PMS toast', take heed. Most of the time, it's not the manager's fault that they can never be found. When we run out of products and supplies, the managers have to walk all the way down to the end of the concourse and down an elevator to replenish the goods. And just in case you couldn't figure it out, Mr. Big guy whose never worked a day in a restaurant, we run out of things at the frequency of a hummingbird's heartbeat!)

Obviously, I couldn't find a manager so I returned to the kitchen. I looked at the pass through window once again for my food, only to notice that the cooks hadn't budged. That's when I broke. I walked into the kitchen and completely lost my head. I yelled at the poor cooks, even though, due to the three different language barriers involved, they probably only understood half, maybe a quarter, of what I said. I think my point was portrayed more so in my body language. A big ass pointer finger in one of the cook's faces while standing about four inches away solved the problem with expedience. As a matter of fact, I haven't seen burritos made that fast before in my life. Go team! I do vividly remember the look on my friends and coworkers faces. They couldn't stop laughing at my episode. They just stared face down at the counter as if I'd never notice them bouncing around as they laughed. I also remember the look of the airport patrons. I think they got a kick out of it too. Most of them were smiling as if to say, "Just give the kid his damn burritos! Come on!" The aftermath of the cooks repeatedly asking me, "Toda via estas enojado con nosotros?" (*You still pissed?), was an acceptable loss. For some reason, though, I didn't get hassled by the kitchen so much any more and they were real careful with their jokes. Well, at least for a week or so. This all just goes to show you; there is no 'i' in team. On a similar note, there is no 'i' in 'donkey' either.

* * *

WHAT THE HELL IS WRONG WITH YOU!?

Now some of the good things: On the other side of the coin, there have been good memories as well. Just in case you are contemplating employment in the field, and incidentally got a copy of this in your hands, I don't want to scare you away from it – at all. I do not regret this path in my life. Matter of fact, I believe the only regrets we have are the things that we were too afraid to do. Sure, I'm bitching like a four year old all the way through this book about the bad, but believe you me, there is quite a bit of good that goes along with this business. The good just isn't funny.

I have literally met millions of people from all walks of life. From bums to businessmen, part-timers to over-timers. In fact, some of my favorite kinds of people are the poorest people you would ever meet that had just enough money to buy a beer. I enjoy their company because of their vast knowledge through his or her experiences.

You meet so many people and hear so many sob stories; it actually helps relieve your stress. Which is a very therapeutic thing for me. It's not that I find pleasure in the misfortune of others that I've talked to; it's just hard for me to always remember that there are other problems on the other side of the bar. When I find out the problems that occur to some of those people out there, God love them, it makes my pathetic little nuisances seem like a day at the beach when it's just too hot. It makes me think to myself, 'big deal, you're still at the beach, kid!'

I've also, mainly at the airport, met quite a few celebrities as well. More importantly, the people that you work with and the clientele that you acquire as 'regulars' become your friends. The friends that I have made in this industry are not just too numerous to list, but priceless as well. The interaction with other people, at times, has had such an impact on me that it has changed my life, usually for the better. All of these people have a story to tell and that's what this business *should* be all about. At least, that's what has made it fun for me all these years.

What The Hell Is Wrong With You!?

* * *

Now that I've explained a little bit about the good and the bad, let's get to the ugly.

I've worked in the restaurant industry ever since I was sixteen years old. I began in restaurants due to my best friend in high school, Nate Ruland. He told me, 'dude, it's the coolest job ever! It's easy, doesn't take much time, and you walk away with money every time you work! Come on! I know the manager. We'll get hired for sure!' He filled me with aspirations of easy money in no time. He wasn't necessarily wrong. After we were hired, I do have to admit, AT FIRST, he was right. He was right about the money, time, and simplicity (if you have the knack). He never told me about being asked to work doubles halfway through my shift. Or dealing with bad management that would tell you to do something and then yell at you for doing it. Nor did he tell me about the stress involved just trying to analyze the stupid things that people say and do. All these things should be common knowledge, but they're not, because people are dumb.

Now, on to the 'doesn't take much time' aspect, I learned my lesson in one very long day. I remember it clearly. I went to school during the day and got to work at about 4pm. At about 8:30pm, nearing the end of a hectic dinner rush, the manger asks me if I could work a double. This would mean that I would work the current night shift, and the following graveyard shift. I made him a deal. If I could go home, take a nap, and then come back at 11 o'clock, I would. He agreed. When I got home, of course, I couldn't sleep because I was still wound up from working. I chose to watch TV and rest. I returned to work at 11, worked all night long, and then went to high school the next day. I think it was about hour number 23 without sleep when deprivation started to take its toll. I started having conversations with Papa Smurf and had this insatiable craving for bacon. I was up for about 30 hours before I just had to go to sleep. It would have been less, but thanks

WHAT THE HELL IS WRONG WITH YOU!?

to Murphy's Law, my car broke down on the way back home from school. Luck of the Irish? Maybe I don't have any Irish in me after all.

* * *

My employment history has been stretched out all the way from fast food to fine dining. At least *they* considered it fine dining. I'm surprised to this day that I have lived through it all! I can tell you the positions I've filled throughout the past ten years. I have been a busboy, cook, bar back, server, bartender, host, cashier, fast food manager, family restaurant night manager, room service attendant, chicken delivery driver, you name it; I've been there. To tell you the truth, 10 percent of my experience is all that was needed for this book. There have been that many idiots.

* * *

Again, a big matter of importance to me is your understanding. If you are offended because you fit the description or profile of a certain character in a story or feel as if you have done 'that' before, then I apologize. Don't feel bad. If, God forbid, you remember being one of the people in a story, feel privileged that you are reading this. Use it as an educational tool. If you do, then you will no longer be laughed, or cursed at in the establishments you go to. I can't speak for everyone in the field, but I'm pretty childish, and kids can be so cruel. I <u>can</u> say that it is a cruel world out there and nobody wants to be the butt of a joke. So watch what you do and say, because you never know who might remember you. It's usually us.

The last thing that I must say about this book has great importance to my morals and I. I want to make it very clear that everyone that has been singled out as an example of a person doing or saying something stupid have not been handicapped, mentally retarded, or foreigners. Picking on foreigners is just too easy. For the others, not only would it be wrong, but also, it would not be

8

very funny. Okay, it could be funny, I guess, but it's still wrong. I'm glad you know this, now we may continue.

Okay! You've now read as much as you <u>need</u> to understand my premise. If not, reread. Just kidding. Hang in there. You'll get it.

The first two chapters are full of stories about some of my working and dining experiences. Most of them take place in prior job settings. However, there are a few stories where I'm not working, but still surrounded by imbeciles. Then we'll get to the really good stuff. The rest of the book includes true stories of stupid customers. Don't get me wrong; they are all pretty funny. They will also give you an idea of what kind of person I am. I was only going to write one or two stories, but I was drunk when writing the chapter and got onto a tangent. The third chapter is when it starts to meld into ridiculous, more recent, slaphappy bar humor. Thank you! Happy reading!

What The Hell Is Wrong With You!?

Chapter Numero Uno:
How Did I Get So Pissed? It Started With 'Jaybeez Restaurants'

It was a long, tedious transgression from a fun loving human being to a bitter rat trapped in a mousetrap struggling to get free. In the beginning, I started this business as a lowly server and progressed from there. When I was 19 years old, I was promoted to management at a family restaurant. I soon moved up to being what they called a Restaurant Manager. That was this chain's way of saying that you worked at night and had to do more work than an Assistant Manager. Yippie. The family restaurant chain that I worked in, we will call Jaybeez Family Restaurants. The one that I managed as an Assistant had a large hotel behind it that we catered parties, ran room service, and also ran a small lounge in the lobby. I learned quite a bit in just a short time working at this one particular restaurant. I learned a lot about growing up too fast as well. I was 19, managed a restaurant, I figured I had it made! They told me that they were going to pay me $375 a week to start. I thought, back in 1993, 'this is great, that's a lot of money!' What they didn't tell me is that I would be expected to work 70 to 85 hour work weeks and be the utility employee that had more to do than simply supervise. Some of these duties included counting money at 2:30 in the morning in an office that had been robbed before, deal with <u>unbelievably pissed off people</u>, chase mice through the dining room, plunge toilets, and many, many other fun tasks. That's also not including all of the other restaurant management stuff that needed to be done.

Also at this time, Jaybeez District Manager was cutting back on labor costs to get his numbers up. We only had two managers in our restaurant. My friend, Gordon, was the General Manager who worked every day (5am to about 3pm). I would then work as the Restaurant Manager every night (3pm to about

2am). Yeah, lots of time to have lots of fun! The only way that we could have a day off is if we called other stores that had three managers, and begged one of them to sacrifice a day off to come in to relieve one of us for a shift. Getting most of these other managers to come to our store, which wasn't the best store in the district, was like getting a bunch of children on Ritalin out of the balls at McDonald's – damn near impossible. So Gordon and I would trade hours. For instance, I would come in at noon so he could leave early. The next day, he would stay late so I wouldn't have to come in until 6pm. It helped a little, but we were still burning out quickly. We did this travesty of restaurant management for three months with about seven days off each. Time off was just another opportunity for sleep, not very 'life fulfilling'. And all this for the low amazing price of $375 a week. A little quick math for you, that winds up being about, ready, $4.86 per hour. Not even minimum wage! Crap, that sucked!

Not too bad so far, right?

* * *

The 'marathon' days, or 'clusterfuck' days, that I have worked were *the most fun*. These were the days when I was 'boss' and everything (and it's mom) would go wrong. I remember when I was, in my own mind, the 'invincible-kid-manager'. I thought that I could handle anything. In one day, my first 'marathon' day, I was put in my 19-year-old place. In one day, everything listed below had transpired:

- ✓ The bartender for the lounge never showed up.
- ✓ One server didn't feel like coming in (I did get to shit-can that person)
- ✓ All the salad bar lights mysteriously went out.
- ✓ One cook called in that morning and no one told me, so the dishwasher had to cook (instant nightmare).
- ✓ The cashier/hostess was a complete idiot (not to abnormal).

WHAT THE HELL IS WRONG WITH YOU!?

- ✓ Mice were running through the dining room that night.
- ✓ The District Manager threatened to show up during my shift (He never did, the putz).
- ✓ Right before close, the heater started to billow out thick gray smoke into the dining room while people were still eating inside.

Some of the normal attributes to your basic hell night. Now the above list is just the tip of the iceberg. The hostess would seat six tables in one section for one server, and two tables in each of the other sections. So the servers would yell at me about it like it was my fault. I'd have to help the slammed sever because there's never any teamwork when there's only one server making money. You know, come to think of it, there is no 'i' in 'screwed' either. I was the only one that could do the room service when all the servers got busy. I also had to help the cook and *dishwasher* cook. I also had to bartend next door at the hotel. When we weren't busy, I had to help the understudy cook catch up on the dishes. I believe it was the very same night that we received an evening food delivery that I was supposed to check in. I think my exact words to the delivery driver were, "You have got to be fucking kidding me! Don't you eat dinner? It's dinnertime! There's about three hundred people in the dining room. I don't have the time to check in an order! Please leave. Leave now."

He had poor time management skills.

Later that night, after the dinner rush, I was quickly changing light bulbs on the exterior of the building, still in fear that the District Manager were to show his gracious presence. On the way to the front door, I was approached in the dining room by one of the patrons from the bar. This woman was a regular (at a hotel bar? Yep, that's sad) and had been drinking a new glass of wine about every 20 minutes or so. She had been in the bar for hours. She looks at me through her squinted eyes and says, "I gustt

WHAT THE HELL IS WRONG WITH YOU!?

warnted u ta know, youv gat to beee the woooorrsssst man, manager that I've, ever seeen."

My only response that I could say, with fluorescent tubes in both hands was, "I'm sorry you feel this way, I wish I could make it better for you." (Smile, walk away.)

Translation: 'Holy shit. You are drunk. Did I do that? Well, I can't care too much about your complaint. You can't possibly be feeling much pain anyhow.' I remember the urge that I had to use those fluorescent tubes on her head like ride symbols in a *Three Stooges* episode. Luckily for her, I was at the beginning of my 'career' and was still in customer satisfaction mode. However if that happened to me now, honestly, I'd just laugh at her slurring. Maybe have her repeat the sentence a couple more times just for my enjoyment. Is that mean? Oh well.

Anyhow, it only took a few of these days in the beginning to knock me off of my 'invincible-kid-manager' pedestal. I'm actually surprised I lived.

WHAT THE HELL IS WRONG WITH YOU!?

DISTRICT MANAGERS AND OTHER SHIT THAT ROLLS DOWNHILL

One of my favorite things that I really enjoyed, were all the meetings and surprise visits from my District Manager. His name was Dan. He was an older, kind of strict guy. He had an east coast accent and an aura of a guy that's not going to take much shit from anyone. Many people found him very intimidating. Not me. Ever since I was in parochial school, I've had a problem with authority figures. I think it was when this nun got upset and threw two handfuls of chalk at the class when we laughed. (She needed to pray for solace a little more, I think.)

This one time in particular, Dan came in with two big-shot corporate people. Sufficed to say, I wasn't really impressed, nor excited about my job, the corporate people, or much of anything else. Anymore. These three people approached me as I stood next to the salad bar. Two of the light bulbs were still burnt out because we didn't have the replacement bulbs in the attic. Working up to 80 hours a week, I didn't care much about the lights; except the flashes of light I saw whenever I closed my eyes. My District Manager decided to throw around a little power and raise his voice to me in the dinning room.

This is a big pet peeve of mine. Like one of my old coworkers, Benny, once said to an old manager of ours, "I'm not your son, I'm not your bitch, and I'm not your dog. If you want to yell at me, you take me to an office!" I never did get to use that line. Well, not yet.

"Now, Freddy, I know I told you to fix these light bulbs last week, why haven't you done it?" My District Manager proudly scolded.

I replied, "I'm sorry, Dan, but we don't have the right size light bulbs upstairs."

WHAT THE HELL IS WRONG WITH YOU!?

He said, looking back to the corporate people with ostentatious mirth, "So then go to the hardware store and buy the right size from petty cash!"

"I would, Dan, but you told us managers specifically not to leave the restaurant without a manager on premise."

"Son, why don't you buy them before your shift on your way into work? I mean, really, what is it that I have to do to get you managers to do anything around here!?"

That's where I lost it, "OH, I'M NOT SURE, DAN, MAYBE GET US A DAY OFF!? YOU KNOW ALL I DO IS SLEEP AND WORK, THAT'S IT, SLEEP, WORK, SLEEP, WORK. SHIT, MAN, I DON'T HAVE THE TIME OR ENERGY TO GO GET THE DAMN LIGHT BULBS. IF YOU'RE SO CONCERNED, WHY DON'T *YOU* GO GET THEM AND I'LL BE PLEASED AS PUNCH TO PUT THEM IN FOR YOU. OKAY!?"

Trying to ignore my panting in anger, Dan puts his hand on my shoulder and says, "We'll get you guys another manager in here real soon, okay?"

After I released, I just stood there like a mad cow staring into nothing. The corporate people, still picking their jaws up from off the ground looked at Dan with disapproval. I was happy to know that my episode would actually get something done to finally help us. We actually did get a new manager in our store. I remember his name was Tim. He eventually extorted a bunch of money from the safe and got fired. As for me, I got transferred to the nice new training store in north Scottsdale where I finally got my days off…and then soon got shit canned.

What The Hell Is Wrong With You!?

I Hate It When I'm Right — How I Got Shit Canned

My first morning in the *training* store happened like this: I got there at 5am to meet the General Manager. I expected a walk through, maybe a couple of hints on how to run this particular restaurant. Yeah, that didn't work.

"Hey, you've managed a restaurant before, right?" He said in his thick Arabian accent.

"Yes, but..."

"Hey, great! Here's the keys, you'll have a delivery at about 10:30, I have an important management meeting (golf) so I'll be back later, about 5. Okay?"

"Uh, I guess..."

By the way, unlike before, if you are reading this and someone offers you a restaurant management position, steer clear! I **am** trying to scare you out of it this time. You should say no before they get out the second syllable in 'management'.

About one year later, my inevitable end of my 'invincible-kid-management' career was becoming apparent. As a poor corporate mistake, I was transferred as an hourly manager when I moved up to the training store. They also paid me on my most recent base salary. Now I was making $425 a week for forty hours, and overtime at $15.95 every hour after that. It was great when I first got there and didn't think of the repercussions. I was a twenty-year-old kid doing the same job as before, with days off, at twice the price. It wasn't so good when the General Manager found out that I was making more money than him. He suddenly made me do the entire inventory, ordering, scheduling, and make up financial proposals for the District Manager. I think he was a little bitter. After he found out that I could handle all of this, I believe he shorted the safe a morning after I closed to make it look like I was stealing. Now, this is only a presumption. I presume

16

this because he was the same manager that I was talking about earlier (Tim) that got fired for extorting thousands of dollars from the company. After having a long talk with the District Manager about my, get this, 'problem with counting', I was pretty perturbed. This signaled the beginning of the end.

A week before I got fired from Jaybeez family restaurants, I was told to begin training one of the long-time servers to be an hourly manager (funny, that's my job!). Everyday for five days I would ask my manager, "Am I training my replacement?"

"No, no, no, no, no, don't be silly, you have nothing to worry about!" He said.

With that, I started typing up my resume.

Guess what! I trained my replacement. How I was let go is such a great story. It really makes you think that when they <u>need</u> a reason to fire you, they'll try just about anything. Here we go.

I go into work for my normal shift on a payday. I walk into the office to notice that my name had been removed from the management schedule. Soon after this, Dan, the District Manager and Tim, the General Manager greeted me for a little closed-door meeting.

"I'm sorry Freddy," Dan said, "but we had to take you off of the schedule."

"Why?" I asked, just pissed.

"It's come to our attention that you were drinking a beer in the office during a dinner rush."

"What!?"

"One of the cooks saw you doing it." The General Manager added.

"I really don't know what the fuck you are talking about!" I yelled as they shielded their faces in fear that the vein in my forehead was soon to rupture.

"Well, the cook that told us is here, would you like to hear it from him?" Dan asked.

What The Hell Is Wrong With You!?

"I'm not saying another fucking word until he's in here!"

I know that didn't make much sense, but I was pissed off. The General Manager opened the office door and called in Dave, the cook. Even if I were guilty, it was the same cook that I would buy alcohol for (yes, I was underage) at the grocery store when we were stuck at the restaurant after last call. What the fuck!?

Dave started with the greeting of a lifetime, "Hey guys, what's up?"

The District Manager asked Dave, "Is it true that you saw Freddy drinking a beer in this office?"

Dave replied, "Uh, I think so..."

I cut in, "You think so!? Did you see me in this office with a beer, yes or no?"

"Well, you were walking towards the office."

"Look at that! I wasn't even **in** the office!" I said to Dan utilizing every muscle in my face to show my emphasis. He didn't like that.

"What kind of beer was it, Dave?"

"It was an O'Douls."

"An O'Douls!?" I said in surprise before continuing my deliberation, "So, I was walking next to the office with an **O'Douls** in my hand. Correct so far?"

At this point, my simple yelling had progressed to a full on scream fest. My face was about as red, I was told, as a neon beer sign emanating in a closet. I think a little twitching may have been involved, but I'm not sure about this.

My incredulity that made me so upset was this: If I was going to jeopardize my job, that I kind of liked at the time; why the hell would I do it with a nonalcoholic beer!? I was underage at the time, so if I were going to drink, I would have gotten stewed! I would have had my own little party, but I guess this logic wasn't apparent to upper management.

WHAT THE HELL IS WRONG WITH YOU!?

After analyzing the situation, I had realized what had happened and found that I will win this battle. I felt kind of bad for the management figures that I was about to put in their places.

"Was this, *O'Douls*, opened or closed?" I asked Dave.

"Well, I'm not sure, I think it was opened," Dave replied.

"Did it occur to you that half of our wait staff is under the age of 19 years old?"

"Well, I..."

"Did it occur to you that in the state of Arizona it is illegal for anyone under the age of 19 to serve alcohol to customers?"

"Yeah, well, O'Douls isn't alcohol." Dave said as he foolishly tried to defend his story.

"Did it occur to you that half of the little kids we have working here don't even know that!?"

"Well, I guess..."

"Have you noticed that the office is adjacent to the walk-in, where we keep the beer, and the dining room, where the customers drink the beer?"

"Yeah."

"Did it occur to you that the only other person here able to serve alcohol to a table that has the time and ability to do so under Arizona law would be me?"

I almost got out one more 'did it occur to you' lines, but I was cut off by the District Manager telling the cook that he could leave the office at the time.

"You've proven your point," Dan told me in a lighter tone, "but you are already off the management schedule (*translation: You're screwed anyway), but I understand that you were a pretty good server when you started with our company. We could put you in any of the restaurants in the district."

It was good to see him back peddling when he knew he screwed up. Point: Freddy.

"I don't want to scrve again." I said.

What The Hell Is Wrong With You!?

"Well you have been trained already, you could be a Kitchen Manager as soon as a position opens up," Dan said, offering another option probably in fear of any possible retaliation from good old Freddy. You know, lawsuit, a complaint to a company big wig, AK-47, what have you.

I ended with, "No, you know, that's okay, Dan. I don't think I want to work for this fucked up company anymore."

I took my check and walked my happy ass out the door. When I left, a couple of servers that heard the whole conversation left with me. I guess they were feeling rebellious. Their own little rage against the machine.

Soon there after, that General Manager got fired. As for me, I did leave Jaybeez for good and went to work for a different fucked up company. Maybe it's fate, it could be luck, but it feels like the combines of the way of the world. The moral of this story: Always stick up for yourself, because in this business, you're probably in the right, but you'll lose your job anyway. Over a son of a bitch nonalcoholic beer. Bummer.

WHAT THE HELL IS WRONG WITH YOU!?

CHAPTER NUMERO DOS: SOME ASSORTED RESTAURANT STORIES ~ FROM BOTH SIDES OF THE TABLE

I needed to add a few of obscure stories in this book so that you can better understand my viewpoint of how I feel about the service industry as a whole. These stories will also help you understand my unique sense of humor.

The first story is about the nervousness involved when you first start in restaurants. It's a funny story that can hopefully help those of you just starting out so that you don't feel alone. The other stories are experiences of mine as I visited, or worked at a couple of my favorite places. For those of you who asked if these stories were going to be in the book, here you go:

SPAGHETTI OLE!

I needed to add this in for all the restaurant employees who, like me, have spilled a tray or two…thousand. For those of you who have never dropped a tray, you are a rare breed, but your day is going to come. A little extra point to throw in for all you new people out there, everybody screws up when they first start. Case in point, I was in high school when I started in the restaurant industry, and I screwed up a lot. Hell, I screwed up <u>everything</u> until I figured out what was going on. I still screw up to this day. Ask any manager. Sometimes other people screw up and just blame it on me because of the rhythm I've gotten into. It was so believable at times; I had to think whether or not I did whatever I was the scapegoat for.

Once, I dropped about ten pounds of frozen peas on the floor. I obtained the entire restaurant's attention. You would be surprised how loud peas can be. I was so nervous and embarrassed, all I could say was, "Oh no! I've *pead* all over the floor!"

Sunday nights, our special would be baked chicken. For quite a few Sundays, some of my tables were asked if they were ready for their 'chicken' as opposed to their 'ticket'.

One of my favorites from when I first started was this: I would get so flustered at times that I would walk up to one of my own tables that had just finished eating and are on the way out the door and say, "Hi, how are you tonight? Can I get you guys something to drink?"

All of these things are awkward and embarrassing, however, dropping a tray is an entirely different story. Nothing else in life can instantly fill you up with fear, remorse, and embarrassment, all at the same time. It's one of those feelings that never let you forget your first time. The feeling is always the same; no matter if it's hot coffee on some poor bastards lap, or a tray slipping leaving $40 in food all over the floor impregnated with shards of porcelain and glass.

Let me tell you about my first time. It was spaghetti night at Heckel's, which was one of the more popular Wisconsin dining specials, next to the fish fry, or course. (If you have ever been to the Midwest, you know what I mean about the fish fry. It's like a religion.) Awkwardly, the trays were rectangular, and the plates were large heavy ovals. You could uncomfortably fit three of these plates on the tray.

It was one of my first days serving, ever. I was busy and nervous. You could just tell by the way the top of my pen shook like my hand was having small convulsions as I scribbled down the order of four spaghetti specials. In my hurry, I did not think much about all the physical properties involved like weight displacement, inertia, gravity, and any other opposing forces at play. I was so hurried that I just threw three spaghettis on the tray and carried the other one by hand. One of my worst favorite tables to wait on was table 25. Table 25 was a large round booth, which was very hard to serve. I had to hold the tray with my left hand and reach all the way over to the inside of the table with my right. This was my problem. That night, I leaned in to set down the plate of spaghetti in my right hand and one of the other plates started to slip off the tray. At the point where I realized that I was not going to be able to salvage it, I slammed the tray into the partition between booth 25 and booth 24. God knows I wasn't smart enough to use a tray jack.

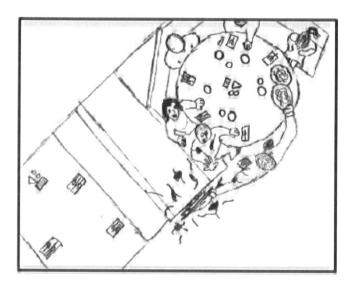

Nothing else gives you the same good feeling as having an entire restaurant staring at you while you hold a tray of food up against a wall. Now, I would probably say, "Oh, I saw a fly." Instead, I was holding the tray there, wondering what to do. The only thing that I could think of saying to the table of partially sauce-splattered patrons was, "Do you mind waiting for different spaghetti? If not, I bet I can salvage this!" I almost cried. They didn't find me too funny. They did eventually get their spaghetti.

* * *

Another memorable time when I lost control of a tray was when a table of eight people all wanted water. At this time, I worked as a server in a big sports bar in Tempe, Arizona. We used plastic cups that were so top heavy when they were full; they were hard to carry without a tray. I pulled off one of the glasses of water and everything seemed okay. The second one, hey, not bad. I picked up the third one and lost balance with the tray. A full 24 ounces of ice-cold water landed on this poor girl sitting nearby. She let out a blood-curdling shriek that silenced the bar and ran to the bathroom. I felt pretty bad. I felt especially bad because I figured I blew my tip. I needed to reconcile this mishap. I took another glass of water and told her to come out onto the patio and throw it on me. I told her, "This is the only chance you will ever get in your entire life to get back at the server that spilled something on you."

Penance was paid in full. I saved my tip, too! So, future reference for all or you out there, sure payback is a bitch, but sometimes it pays off.

* * *

In the past, when I lose a tray, I usually have the tendency to pull the tray into myself so I'm the only one that gets wet. There has been many times where I would be wearing about a gallon of liquid due to this. Because I could never use a tray, I learned how to carry seven cups or glasses, and about seven plates of food without a tray. It looks funny, but it works better. I try to avoid using a tray at all costs now because of how often I spill them. The company that I work for now frowns upon that, but the dry customers appreciate it.

WHAT THE HELL IS WRONG WITH YOU!?

THE SUBWAY STORY

Some would say that this story points out my outgoing personality and sense of humor. Others would just call me an asshole. So be it. It also shows that I will go to great limits of personal humiliation, just for a joke.

One breezy early evening in Phoenix, Arizona, I walked into my neighborhood Subway, one of my favorite places. I walked up to the counter and awaited service. It seemed to be the beginning of their dinner rush, because they were getting a little busy. There were three people working behind the counter. First, the bread, meat, and cheese girl; she was a young teenage high school student who didn't seem to like her job so much. You know, maybe that's not fair. Maybe she was just having a bad day. Regardless, I didn't see any sunshine when she talked to the guy in front of me in line. Next was the veggie guy; he was another high school student, quiet, maintained the flow of sandwich topping, did his job. Then there was the cashier; she was a girl probably in her twenties. She seemed the happiest out of the bunch. As I walked up to the bread, meat, and cheese girl, she greeted me in the normal fashion, except, no smile for me. Boo.

"Welcome to Subway, what kind of sandwich can I get for you today?" She asked in a monotone, almost robotic voice.

"I'll have a foot long Subway Club, on white, with provolone cheese." I stated with a smile as I ordered my usual. She cocked her head, and let out a little sigh in a very sassy way, pointed to a handwritten sign on the glass and began to orally reprimand me for my lack of observation. She had obviously already had to say this about a thousand times so far, so I feel a little bad for what I did, but I couldn't help myself.

"It says right here on this sign that we are out of white bread, we are out of roast beef, and all we have is pepper jack

25

cheese." She scolded in a very authoritative voice. I had no choice but to react abruptly.

"Look lady!" I exclaimed so the whole restaurant could hear me, as I stuttered my breath like I was going to cry, "I can't read! Okay!?"

Everyone in that entire restaurant stopped what they were doing and looked directly at me; and then simultaneously at the bread, meat, and cheese girl. Her jaw dropped faster than the stock market in '29. Silence fell at Subway for just enough time to make it uncomfortable. Then in a slap stick theatrical sort of way, I looked to my right with my arms outstretched and said, "Hey, I'm just kidding folks!"

I then apologized to the poor girl. Luckily for me she thought it was funny. I wound up having a Cold Cut Trio™, on wheat, with pepper jack cheese. In case you wondered, it was very good. I lost 432 pounds. I'm just kidding, I'm very proud of Jared.

WHAT THE HELL IS WRONG WITH YOU!?

THE SOUPER SALAD STORY

Some of my friends have told me that this is one of their favorite stories. Even though there is no conflict between a customer and an employee, it still involves an idiot. I also had a few people request for it to be in here. I'd first like to say that Souper Salad is one of my favorite places in the whole world. For those of you who don't know, Souper Salad is a healthy all-you-can-eat buffet restaurant. Whenever I go, I go through my typical ritual. I have seven trips that are always the same. This is how my routine goes:

1. Regular green salad.
2. Spinach salad.
3. Soup/Chili (sometimes I do the soup group twice, depending on what is prepared that day).
4. Baked potato.
5. Fruit group.
6. Some fashion of bread group usually consisting of angel food cake, cornbread, etc.
7. Last but not least, desserts.

I'm always happy, and stuffed, when I leave there. There was one next to the ASU campus that I would frequent until it closed down. I actually shed tears when I drove by that fateful day to find that the entire building had been gutted. Boo!

One night, my friends, Carrie Chambers, Cindy Nelson, and I went to Souper Salad. I hadn't eaten much of anything that day and was looking forward to my feast. We all walked in, got our first round of food going, and found a table. It was moderately busy that night, but there were no long lines by any means. The time had come for me to get course two underway, the spinach group. Now a spinach salad doesn't need much, therefore I

What The Hell Is Wrong With You!?

shouldn't have been up there a long time. I picked up my new plate and filled it with spinach. I continued down the salad bar when I came across an older man who seemed to be inspecting the cauliflower florets one by one before putting them on his plate. He seemed to be an ASU professor, dressed in a brown corduroy suit with patches on the elbows. Snazzy! After waiting about ten seconds or so, I decided to go around him. He says, "Excuse me, but do you always cut in line like that?"

Confused, I looked around for more people and when I didn't see anybody else, I replied, "I'm sorry buddy, I didn't know that you and I constituted a line."

I looked over at my friends to see if they heard him because he said it pretty loud. They were looking over to see what was going on. I'm one of those people, that if I have an opportunity to make a joke, or an ass out of myself, I will. You may have found that out in the last story. The professor did not respond to me so, under my breath, I let out a little, "okay", and started walking back to his other side where I was before.

"Well you might as well just go ahead now that you've already cut in line!" He blurted out.

Now, this time he was getting a little loud with me. Naturally, I had to do the same back to him. By this time, about a quarter of the people in the restaurant were looking at the two of us, alone at the salad bar, arguing about the line that we weren't. I honestly couldn't tell you if they were looking to see what was going to happen; or looked at me in disgust due to my obvious violation. I could, however, take a good guess. I responded with an exuberant, but polite, "No. Thank you, I'd prefer to wait!"

As the professor moved down the salad bar, I stayed within an uncomfortable proximity as he slowly selected his salad ingredients. I looked around to see other patrons starting to point and jeer at the situation as the professor grumbled to himself like a

WHAT THE HELL IS WRONG WITH YOU!?

grumpy old man. I think he felt a little spite when he found out that all I needed was just a little dressing. That was all. He did get to return to his table about 2 seconds before me, so I guess he got his way, right? He sat about two tables across from us and could hear Carrie and Cindy laughing and carrying on as I told them the story again. But I wasn't done yet. I finished my spinach group and was clearly ready for the baked potato group. When I walked back up for my potato, there was only one guy up at the salad bar. He looked like a student sporting dread locks and getting himself a little salad. I grabbed a plate for my baked potato and walked down the bar. I walked right up behind this guy and in a very cartoon like way, I tapped him on the shoulder. Half of Souper Salad was now looking at me, probably just to see what I was going to do. I cleared my throat and said in a polite, game show host like voice, loud enough for everyone to hear, "Excuse me sir. Would you mind if I broke out of our line and moved on?"

"Why the hell would I care?" He said as he slowly shook his head in disbelief that I was even asking.

As I looked over to the professor, who was now scowling at me from across the room, I made sure he heard me say, "That's what I said! See? It's not me!"

Now the moral of the story is simple: If you want to be a grumpy person, fine, just don't do it on the happy people's time. And I was being nice.

WHAT THE HELL IS WRONG WITH YOU!?

WATCH YOUR BACK, THAT'S HER HUSBAND

This is a quick little story to tell you guys to always be careful what you do at the bar. My first bartending job was at one of the coolest bars I've worked in to date. It's a little bar up in North Scottsdale called Coppers. It was also the second busiest bar that I've worked in as well. Not only did it teach me how to be a quick and efficient bartender, but it also let me understand how much fun it can be on the other side of the bar. We had a large clientele from the surrounding car dealerships. These regular customers would come in every night and drink like there was no tomorrow. Not saying that that was a bad thing. As a matter of fact, I envied them. I can't drink like that and work every morning like those guys did, and probably still do. True troopers they are. Anyway, one of these guys, we'll call him TJ, was in at about 8pm with the normal car salesmen group.

It was pretty much a normal night until this good-looking brunette walked into the bar. Her hair was left to flow and bounce as she walked her tight little dress up to the bar. She sat down by herself and ordered a drink. The car salesmen were looking at her like a bunch of little boys, window-shopping at an old-fashioned toy store – in slow motion. After about 20 minutes of gawking at this girl from the sales team, TJ, I think on a dare, went over and started talking to her. I was pretty sure that all of his buddy's pats on the back and high five's wouldn't help him.

I missed most of the conversation, but they looked like they were doing okay. TJ leads her over to the rest of his crew. TJ introduces her and orders a round of shots. Showing a little (subtle) sexual connotation, he ordered everyone a 'Piece of Ass' (Amaretto, Southern Comfort, and a splash of Sweet and sour, it's pretty tasty). So TJ and this girl started to get a little friendlier with each other. Then, completely out of the blue, they started making out and patting each other down like a couple of cops in

WHAT THE HELL IS WRONG WITH YOU!?

competition. Just before everyone could notice and start throwing all of their drunken jokes to him reality struck. A tall, stocky, Italian looking guy walks up to them and, by their shoulders, breaks them up like a ref in a hockey fight. The girl looks over at the Italian guy, sees that it's her husband, pushes TJ away from her, slaps TJ across the face, and then tells her husband that this guy just grabbed her and started making out with her. Luckily for TJ, I think that the husband was a little to wise to her dramatic cover up. He didn't even look at TJ, grabbed his wife, and walked out the door. I don't know about you guys out there, but I wouldn't know whether to be happy or sad for many, many reasons. Moral of this story: If it seems too good to be true, then she's married.

What The Hell Is Wrong With You!?

Chapter Numero Tres: Warning ~ Bullshit Artists May Be Psycho!

There are so many stories about the bullshit artists that I've run into. There's no way I could possibly tell them all. I don't personally understand the need for some people to lie about what they have done or what material possessions they have. Don't get me wrong; I can empathize and see that it would be fun to pretend. But when you make it so incredibly obvious that you're lying, it makes you look bad – not good. I'm going to tell a few memorable stories about this breed of people.

No Mas Finger

This first story will best point out how the mind of a bullshit artist can work in its own twisted way. When I managed Jaybeez, there was a little, almost albino guy, that worked there as a cook. Just a cook. He would tell everyone stories about how he was in a couple movies and had millions of dollars at his fingertips. The weird thing is that he didn't have a car, but millions of dollars. One night in particular, he just <u>needed</u> to leave work early, but I couldn't let him. After telling me that he doesn't need this job and how he's so much better than this, he returned to the kitchen. I guess he decided to keep working because he was probably saving up money to buy a vault for all of his other money.

I guess he *really* needed to get out of work. I think what he really wanted to do was give himself a small flesh wound that would gush just enough blood for me to say, okay, go home. Instead, he accidentally cut off everything north of the fingernail.

WHAT THE HELL IS WRONG WITH YOU!?

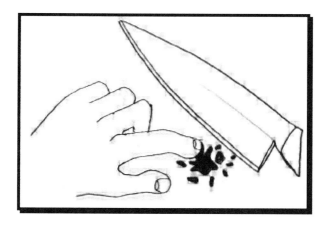

I remember hearing a loud Chihuahua yelp from the kitchen, followed by the clang of a knife hitting the ground. He achieved his goal, he got to leave early, but I don't think going to the emergency room was his initial reason. I'm not really sure what happened to him after that because he never did return to work, but I let *most* of him go (get it?). So do you suppose that would just grow back? Hmm. Point to ponder.

What The Hell Is Wrong With You!?

Started Young ~ Still Needs Practice

Some of the strangest people are bullshit artists. I think what makes the most entertaining artists are the ones that are really bad at it, but think you will believe anything they say. Granted, there are some out there that are good at it, but they're called 'con-artists' and do it for personal gain, not ostentatious pride.

In the bar, just last month, a guy was in that fit the description of the title. The best part was the end when someone else called his bluff. He was a younger kid; I'd say about 22 years old. He was dressed in a dress shirt, loosened tie and a black sports coat. Nothing that seemed too extraordinary at the airport. He was quickly sucking down gin and tonics as if we were about to take his drink away soon. He actually did get to that point too, so I guess he was thinking ahead. He seemed like an okay guy until his, I'd say, third drink. That's when it began. And it usually always begins with money.

"Bartender, could you get us all a round of shots on me, I've got the money, I'm not worried about it." He said to Stuart, the other bartender.

This should have been our first clue. Next, he's a computer programmer that has personally worked with Bill Gates. Sure, it's possible, but I think maybe he just upgraded his Windows® and figured, well, you know.

One of the best parts of his story is when he told a couple of guys out on vacation that he had a patent for a certain popular computer product; and that he's made four million dollars on it already. The other guy at the bar had a constant look on his face as if to be thinking the same as me, 'If this kid has four million dollars, why the hell is he flying commercial?' I know I wouldn't. Hell, I'd just buy my own plane, or ride Bill Gates'.

The kid then ended one of his sentences with a 'what do you think about <u>that</u>!?' Full of vainglorious pride. That's when it happened. One of the guys sitting at the bar said, "It all sounds pretty good, but I think it's all <u>bullshit</u>!"

Everybody that heard just started cracking up, except for the kid, of course. Even I couldn't believe he said that to him. The kid's defenses instantly went up as he tried to justify his story. He pulled out his Michigan license and threw it down on the bar.

"That's my name! I'm not sure what my patent number is off the top of my head, but it starts with four million something something. (That's convincing) Go to ECP.com and look it up for yourself!"

He kept going on and on until the guy at the bar chuckled into his beer and playfully retracted his comment.

Just so you know, at the time, I looked up ECP.com and it *is* a site. But to date, it has not been launched yet. I'm not sure how anyone could look up a patent like that anyway, but what do I know?

Now for the worst part of the story: this guy must have had so much money that he figured he didn't have to pay for his bar tab. He snuck out with a girl that was sitting next to him at the bar. I actually went out to look for him in the concourse and found the girl that he left with. The girl said that she didn't know the guy at all. She also said that he was kind of a freak. Hmm, well, you know what they say about that fine line between insanity, and freaky multimillionaires.

WHAT THE HELL IS WRONG WITH YOU!?

LOOK AT ME! LOOK AT ME!

This one is so outrageous; I had to put it in even though it's short.

One day I was serving at the airport. A man with a small stature spastically ran up to the bar. What I mean by small is about 5'1", maybe 130 pounds soaking wet. One of the first things that he said to the bartender was, "Don't you recognize me? I'm Brad Pitt."

Working at the airport, I do see some celebrities on rare occasions. A couple of examples would be Tim Curry, Bill Watson, Charles Barkley, and the 'grandfather of funk' himself, George Clinton. Some try to hide their identity from the ones around them. Most will be quiet like any other customer and sign some autographs here and there. NOT ONE has run up to the bar to proclaim their stardom. I would also like to believe that Brad Pitt, or any star of that caliber, wouldn't be traveling alone.

Anyway, we were all very sure that he was joking. He wasn't joking. I don't know if it was an actual mental dysfunction with this guy, or just plain bullshit. Soon after he stated his prominence, he left the bar. Coincidentally, I walked out to the concourse towards one of the airlines' customer service counters to ask them an unrelated question. I saw the little guy run up to the counter in front of me. I then quickened my pace to see what he would tell them.

"Could you do me a favor?" He asked the airline employee behind the desk, "Could you page a Mr. Brad Pitt to gate A17? Thank you."

Right after he said that, he didn't walk, but sprinted back to gate A17. I didn't follow him, but I would guess, someone didn't believe his story so he had himself paged. That would be good enough proof for me, for sure! I mean, come on, only doctors and movie stars get to have their names paged on intercom systems.

What The Hell Is Wrong With You!?

The Tale Of Mr. Gold And "Scooter"...Super Vendor!

This started out as a story about a guy that was waiting for his flight at the airport. His name is Scooter. He sat down at the end of my bar while I was cleaning near the end of my shift. Then, Mr. Gold, who was in earlier, returned to the bar and sat next to Scooter.

When Scooter first sat down, he seemed to be a very strange individual. Just in case you are reading this, Scooter, keep going; you wind up being the good guy. I didn't think him to be weird in appearance, more so in actions. It looked like maybe he had a couple before he came in.

As I was cleaning down my well and putting away bottles, he started asking me questions about everything that I was doing. He wanted me to break down my side work to him, play-by-play. Not too strange, not yet. I use a speed opener for bottled beer that to a lot of people, that have never seen one before, find the procedure of opening a beer fascinating. Scooter seemed to almost fit in this category. He asked me about it, and how I did it, and how I learned. I went along, answered all of his questions. Everything was fine. He then told me that he was traveling to do a similar gig in a different state. I asked him what it was, and he said that he was a baseball park vendor. While I was holding back on saying anything about the obvious, and gigantic differences between bartending a full bar in the airport verses selling beer in a ballpark; he busted out his business card.

WHAT THE HELL IS WRONG WITH YOU!?

"**Scooter**" ...*Super Vendor*

Attaboy!

BEER LINE:

www.scooterattaboy.com

As you can see above, that's his card. He then spontaneously gave me an example of how he sells beer. I think we all know, "Heeeeey, git yer Coor's Light, Coor's Light here, coold ice cold, cold Coor's Light here, beer here, beer!!!"

I do have to say, he does it a lot better than me. It felt like I was at the ballpark. He also got the attention of everyone else in the bar. He tried comparing our jobs by how we open bottles of beer. Though shocked that I had actually heard of plastic beer bottles at the ballpark, he proceeded to mime how he hits the lids off so they shoot up in the air and he catches them. Usually I open the bottles with a flat metal opener and catch the caps on their way down. Though completely different, he figured they were exactly the same. What?

The weirdest thing that this guy did was this: While I was cleaning my well, he would spurt out a, 'You know what they say...' and leave it at that. I would stop what I was doing to find out *what they say* only to find silence.

The first couple of times, I figured maybe he was just watching television and thinking really loud. I do it sometimes, usually while I'm watching hockey games. My language is usually quite coarse. I am calling Scooter a little weird, only because I am too. I, myself, am a firm believer in intra-personal communication on a day-to-day basis. It helps to maintain my mental well being, because, shit, if you can't be your own friend, then whose friend **can** you be?

Hang in there, Scooter; your good guy part is still coming up.

Now the other character has a little history to be told of his strangeness. He was in the bar earlier that evening before meeting Scooter. Let me take you back about one and a half hours prior. I couldn't figure out what this guy's deal was as soon as he started talking. He was a bigger, Italian looking guy who sat by himself at the middle of the bar. He wore a black sweater that emphasized his oversized gold chain necklace. And when I say oversized, I mean you could tow a boat with that puppy. We will refer to him as Mr. Gold. Mr. Gold was multiple times stranger than Scooter. When he first sat down, he just seemed to be another weirdo. When he came back later that same night, it became so much worse. In the past, I've been pretty good at picking up on this stuff, but my idiot-o-meter must have not been working properly the first time I met Mr. Gold. One of the first things that he said to me, after I served him his first beer, as he held the glass up in cheers, "Here's to six years of sobriety!"

Okay...

Now, I don't want to be the cause of anyone's downward spiral back into a 12-step program, but, legally, I have to serve him until he's breaking the law.

That should have thrown me off a little, but I just looked at the other bartender, Stuart, who heard him. Stuart was already looking at me shaking his head in dismay. That's were it remained. I carried on conversation with Mr. Gold just like a normal person you would find in the bar. Halfway though one of my favorite stories (if you hadn't noticed, I like to tell stories) an older-than-middle-aged woman sat two seats down from him. I was still telling my story when I asked him if he would like another beer. He said "yes," and in a very smooth, yet cheesy way, he added, "and get whatever that lovely lady down there would like."

The lady said thank you and moved down to his side. As I made their drinks, I noticed that they started talking about their flights in kind of a secretive manner. It's hard to 'not help overhear' when I'm eavesdropping. Anyway, I set their drinks down and started washing glassware. I also continued where I left off with my story. When I looked up a couple minutes later, I noticed that they were paying no more attention to me. I mumbled to myself about how I was just telling a story and how it wasn't important anyway.

They talked for about an hour when Mr. Gold started inching himself closer and closer to the girl.

Now, just to throw in a point, if you meet a girl at the airport, and things start to work out for you, cool. I wouldn't say no, most guys wouldn't. It's actually happened to me before. Except my story involved a gorgeous little blonde girl named Amber, Las Vegas, and a super-spontaneous mid week vacation. I needed the time off anyway. Too many burritos. However, in Mr. Gold's case, I would have a hard time doing anything with a woman that reminded me of my mother. This woman could have been his mother. Age wise, that is, otherwise I would expect them to recognize each other.

Mr. Gold moved in for the kill. Every inch he leaned in muttering, "just a kiss, just lemme kiss you," she would inch back a little further. So I was washing glassware, nonchalantly looking on to see if Mr. Gold goes up like a roman candle, or down like King Kong from the Empire State Building. Right before she reached the brink of 'if I back up anymore I'll be laying down' (maybe his idea), she kind of muttered a, "well, okay," then gave in. I shuttered a bit, and then stuck my head in the three-compartment sink. They soon tabbed out and left the bar. I just figured that they were on the same flight and were going to their gate. Never did a spank-happy toilet stall sex session cross my mind. I honestly can't tell you that's what had happened either, I just said it never crossed my mind. It couldn't. Not with those two. Yuck.

About an hour and a half later, Mr. Gold reappears. At this time, Scooter is already at the bar saying things like, "You know, that's something I really like..." and leaving it at that. Again, I'm just cleaning my well. Mr. Gold's six-year sobriety party was obviously into full force. Unfortunately, now it was a solo party and the woman had gone. He seemed to glow, so you can all draw your own sick little conclusions, because I know I have. He sat down at the bar and started talking to Scooter. I started feeling sorry for Scooter, because every time Mr. Gold addressed him, he'd screw up his name. Scooner was his most favorite. There were others like Scooper, Scraper, etc. Every time Mr. Gold would say this, Scooter, really leaving sobriety at this point would slowly exclaim, "It's SCOOTER!!"

Mr. Gold didn't seem to care about his name. He was probably too concerned about how great he was and whatever story he was telling to whomever. I will have to admit, though, Mr. Gold was very personable. New people would sit down at the bar and be greeted by Mr. Gold before anyone working at the bar.

As it got closer to closing time, which in our airport is around 11pm, thank God. Mr. Gold and Scooter were approaching the point where they would need to stop drinking if they wanted to ride on a plane. Mr. Gold tells me that he's going to buy half the bar a round of shots. I figured, okay, but that's the last I was going to serve them. Scooter was at the point that I bargained with him to give him a Corona instead of a shot of tequila. I did this because he already had a few shots in the past <u>hour</u>. That's a good example

WHAT THE HELL IS WRONG WITH YOU!?

of how they were at that point. I told someone else at the bar that their tab total was nineteen ten. Mr. Gold, with great fear in his eyes yelled, "What time is it!?"

What I don't get about that is it was about 10:45. What the hell did he think I said? Military time would have made it only 7:10. Maybe in his world there is a *19 o'clock.* I don't know.

Then, completely out of the blue, Mr. Gold became a stereotypical bullshit artist. He looked over to the patrons to his right. The same strangers that he greeted and bought shots for just in the past ten minutes. With arms sprawled across the bar, he stuttered, "I bet. I'll bet you, that last year, that I paid more in taxes last year, than you grossed all year long."

It always has to have something to do with money!! The couple looked over with very surprised looks on their faces. I was thinking – how could a drunken mind have the reason to put that sentence together...then exclaim it. The couple looked as if they were thinking the same, but found it comical and played along.

The woman returned, "Okay, how much did you pay in taxes last year?"

There was a big, long pause before he lethargically answered, "$41,000!"

I literally dropped the speed rail's liner and cocked my head in the traditional confused puppy dog look full of wonder and disbelief. Everyone, including Scooter, slowly turned back around to his or her original positions in disbelief. The greatest part was when Mr. Gold just giggled to himself as to say, "What? What's wrong?"

Not only is that the single stupidest that you could *ever* say, it would be so much worse if it were true. Just think of all the questions that would arise. What kind of worthless accountant could this guy have? And if he did pay that much, why the hell is he at the airport waiting for a delayed flight? Why would he have to hit on the older ladies? I mean, if you made enough money to need to pay $41,000 in taxes, you would have a girlfriend. I know I would. I don't know though; I'm not too smart.

This is where you get the props Scooter. The time had come for everyone to leave. Mr. Gold tossed me his credit card. I ran it through and brought back the slips. On the slips, it says the subtotal, leaves space for a tip, then a line for the total; just like any credit card slip in just about every bar or restaurant in America. He crossed out the tip line and totaled it out without a tip. With all of the shots that he bought for everyone else, his tab was about $40. Scooter looked over and said, "Aren't you going to leave them a tip?"

Mr. Gold said, "No, he doesn't need a tip."

Anyone at this point that agrees with Mr. Gold, stop reading here. Please finger ahead to chapter number eleven, labeled 'Tipping'. Throughout the years, tipping has been a misunderstood and misconstrued thing that I will break down for you. Everyone else, go ahead:

Scooter replied, "Yeah he does. These people live on tips!"

Mr. Gold, God bless him, gave Scooter the stopping bus noise, you know, the piusssshhhhhhh, and exclaimed, "Later Scooner!"

Which was returned with, "It's SCOOTER!"

Scooter looked around and noticed that I listened to the whole thing as I yelled out my exuberant thanks to Mr. Gold. He reached in his pocket and pulled out about $15. He gave it to me and apologized for Mr. Gold's rude behavior and told me that he understands.

The moral of the story: The people that tell everyone around them that they have a lot of money will probably not tip. The ones that do have a lot of money won't say anything about it, and tip huge. Then everyone else will be explained in chapter eleven. Last but not least, the people who are in the industry are the coolest people in the world. If any of you out there run into

WHAT THE HELL IS WRONG WITH YOU!?

Scooter at a baseball game, be sure to throw him a little bread, he works hard for you. Thanks Scooter!

* * *

All in all, I love talking to bullshit artists just because they make me laugh. I once had a guy that came into Old Chicago on a bicycle. He told me that he 'made up' all of the signals that baseball coaches use. He also told me that he instructed football coaches and baseball pitchers to cover their mouths when they talk so lip readers from the other team wouldn't know the upcoming plays. (Wait a second! Didn't I also see that on *Casino*? Oh, well.) Then, he suddenly became overwhelmingly aesthetically mesmerized with the graphics on the front of the menu. He couldn't stop saying how beautiful it was. Don't get me wrong; it was a cool menu, but it was just pictures of beer bottle labels. Nothing to get too excited over. Also, it's nothing that you couldn't make yourself through time and beer. He had me ask the manager to see if I could sell it to him. After telling my manager the whole story, he told me to just give it to him so the 'fruit would leave'.

* * *

I had another guy in that same bar in waiting for his wife. This guy was phenomenal. He seemed to be in his 50's and wanted me to go bartend at the VFW. He figured it would have been a better gig for me because I would make $5 and hour and like $20 in tips a shift! He didn't figure that I made much in tips in a real bar. Not only did he also have a couple million dollars in the bank, but he also had worked for the CIA, the FBI, and was also a US Marshall, and he frequents the VFW. One of his best attributes was not something he had, it was something he lacked...his teeth. All but about two. Again, if I had a million dollars and two teeth, I think I would do something about it. Call me silly.

* * *

WHAT THE HELL IS WRONG WITH YOU!?

We will always run into these individuals, and even though it's funny, weird, and sometimes scary, there's no getting away from them. Don't get me wrong; I think exaggeration is a wonderful conversational tool. I just don't call it that anymore. There's a famous quote that Chi Chi Rodriguez once said that I go by, "I don't exaggerate, I just think big." God bless you. I'm sure that's all these individuals are doing, they're just thinking way too big.

OKAY, ENOUGH PLAYING AROUND. NOW WE'LL GET TO THE GOOD STUFF:

What The Hell Is Wrong With You!?

Chapter Numero Cuatro: So, You've Obviously Never Been To A Bar Before

I want to start off by telling everybody that if you go into a bar or restaurant and are greeted by a bartender or server, after a generic greeting, you will be asked a question. The first question that they will probably ask you is if you would like something to drink. I know it's hard to believe. I've never been a big fan of repeating myself, especially when it's busy. It takes up too much time. I probably have about eighty people per shift that respond to, 'Hey, what can I get for you?', with, 'Huh?'. Safe assumption people. Most of you probably don't do this, but for the love of God, if you know someone who does, tell him or her to quit it, seriously. I know that it's a nit-pickity thing, and I apologize. It's a big peeve of mine.

I'm positive that everyone has been to a restaurant before. I'm guessing that everyone reading this book has been to a bar before. It's a pretty safe assumption that almost everyone over the age of 19 has been to a bar before. I know that's when it all started for me. As a matter of fact, most of the people that I talk to, even if they are strangers to me, have had some kind of bar-going experience in one way or another – no matter their age. However, most of the situations that I have in this chapter actually make me second-guess my stereotypes.

First off, it should be a given that when you go into a bar or a restaurant, it's set up for you, the customer. Even at the airport, it's all the same. There is a certain etiquette that you should follow. If you do not know what this etiquette is, then this is the chapter for you.

The breakdown goes like this: You walk into a bar. You have, of course, the bar with the bar stools. If there are more than four tables in the bar you walked into, chances are there are one or more servers to assist you at those tables. No matter where you sit

WHAT THE HELL IS WRONG WITH YOU!?

in a bar, you will be helped. Sometimes there are games, pool tables, darts, a jukebox, neon lights, and customers just hanging out. Now, if you were to walk into a restaurant, you should expect a host person or at least a sign saying to seat yourself. In a bar, you should not need to expect these luxuries. A good rule of thumb to decipher the difference between the two is this: If you walk into an establishment and the largest item that takes your attention is the bar, chances are you're in a bar.

For those of you wondering why I'm taking so much time to explain the difference between the two needs to understand that there are people out there that obviously don't have a clue.

This chapter also goes out to the people who have been to a bar before, but haven't been to a *busy* bar before. For instance, if you go to a bar in the airport when it's busy, and you leave half a plate of food and a quarter of a beer sitting on a table to go check the score on the game on the television **ten feet away**, you may not have your table when you return. You will not have your food or your beer either. One of the most important points that I could ever give about being in a busy bar is this:

✓ **ALWAYS**- Leave a cocktail napkin on top of your drink when you leave it, even if only for a short time.

You would not believe how many drinks are thrown away and wasted because the bartender or server is so busy that they figured you just walked out without paying. What's more, when you return to reclaim your drink with your 'Um, excuse me, um, someone threw away my drink.' You have to go through the whole process again, wasting valuable time of the server's, bartender's, and your own.

What The Hell Is Wrong With You!?

Don't Stand In A Walkway! It Makes You Look Stupid!

Now that I have that out of my system, I will carry on. And yes, again, it's a peeve of mine.

One of my favorite sayings that I've said since I've started serving is, "Please don't stand in a walkway, it makes you look stupid!"

Granted, I had to slowly graduate to this saying, but I'll tell you, some of these people just don't understand. This applies to bars and restaurants alike. If you walk in and just stop while you're walking, either you're going to get a tray gouged in your back, or someone like me will get upset and say something to make you feel dumb. One of the most memorable situations that I could bring up in my experience is from a busy sports bar called McDuffy's in Tempe. On a busy football Sunday with a home game four blocks away, there would be upwards to 700 people in the bar. Now, common knowledge should tell one that there are going to be people that need to get through. Sure as shit, there were always 30 to 40 people on these busy shifts that would walk in using the 'baby steps' of transportation and stop right before the server well and lethargically stare at the televisions around them. Just so you know I'm not a complete bastard, I paid especial attention to what they were looking at. Usually, there was nothing important happening on any of the TVs. The games would be in between plays or it would be a commercial. I understand that the televisions are the draw to this particular bar; however, there is no need to stand in a walkway to check it out.

At this bar, we gave out maps at the front door to show the customers where each game was going to be shown so they had the opportunity to have a clue where they were going. These maps were very self-explanatory and very easy to read. The bar is a large rectangle. There's a big rectangular bar in the middle. The

WHAT THE HELL IS WRONG WITH YOU!?

main room is in the main opening of this bar. You don't have to be a practicing topographer to figure it out. More often than not, people would stand in the walkway next to the bar and stare at the map, then at the sky. No matter what I did or said to help these people, and yes, I tried, they would just stand there, in my way. It was like they were at a stargazing show at your local planetarium, drunk.

At one time, I thought that this phenomenon was only conceivable at a bar that had seventy or so televisions. Boy was I wrong. Working at the airport has shown itself to be worse than I could imagine. Keep in mind that legally, in most airports, these bars are some of the only places you're allowed to smoke a cigarette before you get on an airplane. I'm sure that we are all familiar with the rental luggage carts at the airport. I cannot believe the amount of people that come into the airport bar with this cart full of luggage when we are just slammed, and stand right in the middle of the only available walkway to smoke their cigarette like they are the only person there. I know what some of you are thinking. This guy (me) must not be a smoker, but on the contrary, I used to smoke like a junkyard tire fire and still consider myself an occasional smoker. So I do understand getting in that last cigarette before you take a four-hour flight. I feel the pain. I also have an answer on the next page to help everyone with this dilemma, because really, I just want to help us all get along.

Now, for the non-smokers that walk in halfway between the doorway and the bar and just look around at whatever the hell you could look around at; this doesn't look good for you. I will admit, for an airport bar, our company, 'BFD post', has some good-looking bars. There's a lot of stuff that you can just stare at and enjoy the art side of it. Just please don't do it in the walkway! You too can follow the solutions that I've written in below.

These should be things that everyone should know. I'll even extrapolate it into a few different situations for you – for

WHAT THE HELL IS WRONG WITH YOU!?

better understanding. Would you walk into a church during the sermon and walk halfway up between the pews and the preacher and just stand there and stare at the stained glass? Or maybe walk into a movie theater, walk up next to the screen in front of the first row and just stare around at the speaker system? No! I didn't think so. This isn't that much different. You go to all of these places to complete a function. In many situations, if you were to hang out in places of high traffic or public observation and just stand around in the way, you could put your safety in a great deal of jeopardy. In my case, you're just pissing me off. If you feel the need to stand, that's okay. All you have to do is follow the directions of the 'hero-to-noncombatant' line in any Steven Segal movie, "When you walk, walk against the wall, if you see someone, become part of the wall." This is your answer! Just so you know, if you stand next to any large immovable stationary object, you'll be out of the way. That is unless your server can walk through walls. Thanks Steve.

WHAT? YOU CAN SEE THROUGH WINDOWS?

One of my worst favorite things that have happened everywhere applicable is when people crowd a doorway to watch television. These are the people that don't want to come in, sit down, maybe have a drink or something, and enjoy the game. They are the people that will stand in the doorway for literally an hour or so to watch the game that's on the television inside. As shown in the diagram, it's even better when you are a server that needs to get in and out of those doors because there are patio tables. I would then use a variation of my already favorite saying, "Please don't stand in a doorway, it makes you look stupid!"

WHAT THE HELL IS WRONG WITH YOU!?

Usually people are like, "uh, okay", and move out of the way until I walk through. Then they will conjugate back to their original positions. One of the funniest things that I can't figure out is this: As shown in the diagram, at the bar that I work at, on both sides of both doorways, there are 6 huge 9-foot by 5-foot panes of glass that no one would ever look through. They just stand in the doorway. Why!? Does the glass somehow distort the game or disturb their viewing pleasure? I don't get it. I really can't see how hard it is to understand the complexities behind transparent walls, but people would never use them.

Actually, I need to retract that. They would use the 'magic transparent walls' after we had closed, or before we had opened whenever we had a game on the televisions. They would actually line up on the glass like a hundred exotic salt-water fish trapped in an oversized fishbowl. It was rather amusing.

* * *

Another one of my favorite things about knowing the difference between a bar and a restaurant is more evident at the airport than anywhere else I have ever worked. Granted, any service industry based establishment *should* have some sort of person to greet the customer. I agree with this unless it's a bar, and just a bar, especially at the airport. When you go to a bar and there is no one at the door, waiting for someone to help you is kind of pointless.

There have been times that I've been so busy I didn't know whether to crap myself or swallow my own tongue. I would run frantically to the computer terminal to ring in about twelve or thirteen orders of drinks and food while trying to stay focused. At times, more frequent than you would believe, I would find in my peripheral vision, anywhere from two to five people just standing in the doorway, pissing me off. Not only at the main doorway, but the smaller one to the side. Big smiles on their faces as they watch the chaos go by them like a monorail train just opened at Disney World™ and was making it's inaugural pass across the front entrance. Big smiles. So of course, half of it being my job, and the other half not being able to work effectively knowing that they exist there, I say, "It's all seat yourself folks, just help yourself, go ahead," as my head remains buried in the computer terminal. One or two, depending on how many of there are, would let out a little, "Oh, okay," and then slowly enter into the building, just looking around, further throwing me off my train of thought. Now that the train of thought has been completely derailed, I have to start the whole process over again. And I would probably wind up waiting on them, too.

What The Hell Is Wrong With You!?

Red Square Tables

I put this passage here because it definitely classifies itself as one of those things that shows proof positive of intelligence here on earth. When it's busy and this happens, I usually only have time to grind my teeth in repugnance. The other times it happens, I just have fun with it.

"Excuse me, but, where is your smoking section located?" A voice would ring off the side of my weeded head.

"You can smoke at all the red, square tables."

Did everyone understand the quote I just wrote? It astonishes me how many people in this world have the hardest time understanding that simple line. I've had people just kind of nod their heads and wander into non-smoking where the tables are round and stone. Hey, I can't get too mad, they got one out of three! They are tables. Not bad, good show. I've had people stop to analyze it and murmur to themselves, "red, square, okay."

"Are those the red, square tables?" The girl from above asked me as she pointed to the half of the restaurant completely full or red, square tables. I stopped what I was doing to stare at her bubbly ignorant smile and ask her what she had just said. I was hoping that she would process it in her own head, but she didn't. She repeated herself, but giggled a little after the second time.

* * *

One of my favorite comebacks to this was when a younger lady walked into the bar and asked if smoking was permitted in the bar.

"Sure," I replied, "red, square tables and up at the bar."

"Just up at the bar?" She asked.

"Yes, just up at the bar." Obviously showing that it was just too hard for her to process all the information and just go with the easier of the two options.

What The Hell Is Wrong With You!?

I mean seriously, we are dealing with basic shapes and colors here. Maybe it's been that long for people who have only used those kinds of hi-tech skills in the first grade and have abandoned it and left it behind (like algebra in high school).

Pulling The Wool Right Over Our Eyes!

While I'm on the subject of smoking sections, I'd like to point out another absurd idiosyncrasy that people have done numerous times. It usually happens when we are pretty busy and most to all of the tables in smoking are full. In non-smoking, there are signs on every table that say: Nonsmoking Section. Pretty self-explanatory. 'Non', meaning 'no'; 'smoking', meaning 'the use of flammable tobacco products'; and 'section', meaning 'area'. Pretty simple. Now I know that half the people that say, "Oh, I didn't notice, I'm sorry," are lying through their teeth. These are not the people that crack me up. It's the people that notice the sign, sit down, light up a cigarette anyway, and **turn the sign around so it's just a blank piece of paper!** What the hell is this!? Do these people really think that without the sign, the employees would just forget which tables are smoking and which are not? Some even have the tenacity to ask you for an ashtray as you walk by. I'll tell you what, for the people out there that think this works, try this: The next time you get pulled over for speeding, grab a big roll of duct tape and put it over your instrument panel. When the cop comes up to your window, simply tell them that you couldn't see your speed; therefore, you could not have been speeding. See if that works out for you.

WHAT THE HELL IS WRONG WITH YOU!?

BAR JARGON

This one could explain why I have printed a glossary of terms in the back of this book. This example doesn't happen all too often, but I still find it rather amusing. I'll run across this breed of people that don't seem to say what they mean about twice a month (luckily).

For better understanding of why this particular quark bothers me, I will explain a few things about wasting extra, unwanted drinks. First off, it's a waste of alcohol. Being a big fan of alcohol, this is a personal strife between myself, and the person who's wasting it. Secondly, it becomes a waste of time for the bartender, the server, and/or any other employees involved. Granted, it's about 15 to 30 seconds of time, however, over a lifetime span, this could add up to almost 12 hours of my life – gone forever. And last, not to mention the added time used off of my life as a whole, but the pain in the ass of the process of handling a void at the bar that I work at now. Normally, all you would need is a manger to fix the ticket. Here, however, if you have a void, no matter how busy you are or how large the ticket is, you must always follow the same procedure. The procedure is to print out the ticket, write 'VOID' on the ticket, cash out the ticket, make a new ticket, apologize to the cooks or bartenders if you forgot to hit the 'Don't make' key after re-ringing everything you now have double of, and then void off the entire old check. Here's the clincher! The manager does have the ability to void off one item at a time on a check (line item void), but thanks to the company, they're not allowed to. So hence, the procedure.

It's really good to work for a company that doesn't trust its managers. Not very logical? Try this one on: This is the same company that actually had to have a meeting, discuss and agree not to display clocks in their bars...AT THE AIRPORT! I know this as fact because the employees of 'The Tequila Place' put a clock on the shelf behind the bar once, only to have it taken down by a corporate manager. It's against policy.

Anyhow, back to my original gripe. I had a table of two people drinking bloody marys. The man said exactly this, "Hey, could we get another round and the tab?"

I brought them two more bloody marys and their check. Why wouldn't I?

They said, "No, we only wanted one more drink." Again, with the expression that it was my fault. When I told him that he ordered a 'round', he didn't see how that was confusing. I took the second bloody mary back to the bar and told the bartender what had happened. When I went through the process of a void, I didn't hit the 'don't make' button because I just told the bartender what happened. To show, once again, that we are all human, the bartender made three new bloody marys. The moral of the story: When you order a 'round' of drinks, and you're not by yourself, you will get more than one drink. See glossary.

What The Hell Is Wrong With You!?

Bars Lack Host-people

If you think that there's more about the 'should know' in knowing the difference between a restaurant and a bar, you're absolutely correct! I cannot stress this point enough because it really makes people look stupid. I started talking about it before in the beginning of the chapter, but I feel the need to go in depth for the people way in the back that can't hear me very well.

Again, it's a safe assumption that if there is a person, usually a teenager, sitting at a podium, they are there to seat you. There are basically two types of hosts/hostesses/greeters. Both are relatively easy to spot:

There is the first, and more common breed of host, the slacker. This will be the person doing homework, or the crossword, or their nails (male or female, welcome to 2001!) that, if they are not to troubled by your presence, will get up and seat you. This is really good seeing that they are the first person to greet the guest, but that's just marketing.

The other kind is from the opposite side of the spectrum. This will be the host-person that *is* genuinely happy to see you. They will smile and immediately approach you to find a solution to your every seating need. That job is the single most important thing to them, next to getting their drivers licenses. They take their jobs more seriously than anyone else in the restaurant. They remind myself of a younger me. Back when I cared so much about the happiness of the guest, no matter what cruel and unforeseeable things they did to me.

IF THERE IS NO PERSON IN THE FRONT, chances are it's seat yourself. Most bars in America are like this. I know, I've been to plenty and remember most. If you do decide to wait in the doorway, expect to wait a very long time. There, I feel better now. Again, thank you.

What The Hell Is Wrong With You!?

It's Hard To Stray Off The Beaten Theme

Unlike your typical stereotype of an airport bar, they are becoming nicer and more enjoyable. Take our bar for instance. We are calling it 'The Tequila Place', which is a branch of 'PMS Toast'. Like I mentioned briefly before, it's decorative and Mexican in theme. This could explain the Mexican name, the Mexican food you smell, the Mexican tiled floors, and the Mexican looking artifacts on the walls. Now, without jumping to the answers right away, I want you to read the question, then close your eyes and think of the answer. Keep your hand over the answers on the right side, and remember, no peeking!

- Knowing what you've read above,
  what kind of food do we serve?.......................Mexican

- What kind of beer do we have
  the most of?...Mexican

- What would you think our
  specialty drinks are?...............................Margaritas

- What spirit do you think we
  specialize in?..Tequila

How'd you do? Sorry, I know I didn't tell you that there would be a test. I'm hoping that maybe you got at least a 75 percent score. Relax, that's passing. The reason you had this test was to see if you fit this category of people. Hot dogs are not a Mexican delicacy. No, we don't serve French fries with our tacos.

One of my personal favorites is when someone asks if we have margaritas. Some even ask if we make good margaritas. First off, if I were bartending, I would be the one making the drink.

What The Hell Is Wrong With You!?

I'm not going to say, "Yeah, try one, it'll suck!" Secondly, with our theme in mind, wouldn't it just occur to you that, yes, we probably have mastered the skill behind mixing tequila and sweet and sour? I just don't get it.

What The Hell Is Wrong With You!?

Okay Kids ~ What Airport Has A Winery?

There also seems to be some sort of confusion that also doesn't quite fit the theme of an airport bar. You are not in a four star resort. There are many differences (the big shiny airplanes should have been your first clue). For instance, our selection is very limited, while a four star resort has pretty much everything. If they don't have what you want, they'll probably go get it for you. We won't.

No matter how hard I try not to, I find myself laughing at the person who says this; "May I see your wine list?"

This is a perfect example of someone who hasn't grasped the reality that they are in the airport. My answer is usually, "Sure, I actually have it memorized – red or white?"

When they ask what kind it is, I follow with, "Well, frankly, I'm not sure what it is *this week*, but I can tell you it comes in a really big bottle."

We are also thankful to have the opportunity to come across the real uneducated wine connoisseur. They're the ones that will ask what kind of red wines we have chilled. I think I've said 'Boonze'.

* * *

I was recently at my local watering hole talking to an employee of a familiar chain restaurant down the street. He and I were talking on the subject when he shared one of his choice one-liners to a customer about wine.

"What's the difference between a white wine and a dry wine?"

He replied, "I think the answer is hidden in the question."

That probably left the people dumbfounded enough to just order a Coke. Props to Robert for that one, thanks brother.

What The Hell Is Wrong With You!?

Chapter Numero Cinco: What's On Tap, Besides The Obvious?

This is probably going to be my favorite chapter, you are all entitled to choose your own, but I'll bet this is going to be at least a bronze in your mind. I'm going to start with something that happens all of the time. This is by far one of the funniest things that I've ever seen. What makes this so funny to myself, and all of the other bartenders, is that it's the truth. I'm not talented enough to make up such craziness. I kid you not when I say that this 'happens all of the time'; it's not like a one-time fluke. I've personally seen this happen about 20 to 25 times in the past three months. And no, I'm not just 'thinking big'. Look at the picture and imagine this person saying this, "Yeah, uh, could you tell me what you have on tap?"

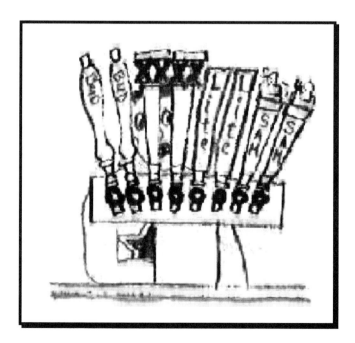

What The Hell Is Wrong With You!?

At the bar that I work at now, there are four beers on tap. The tap handles come strait out from the middle of the bar. People literally stand eight inches from the tap handles and ask that. They couldn't be closer to the handles without sitting on top of the bar. Just when you thought it couldn't get any *stupider*, it does. Now that you know the basic setup of the taps, you will fully appreciate this story that a couple other bartenders at my work told me about.

A man walks up to the bar, smack dab in front of the tap handles (see picture again, if needed), while fighting to see through the tap handles, he asks, "Yeah, what do you guys have on tap?"

Brandon Sirstins looks at the tap handles like he is reading them for the first time and says, "Looks like, Dos Equis, Sam Adams, Bud, and Miller Lite."

"Do you have Fosters?"

In amazement, Brandon slowly double checks the four beers at there handles again and says, "Nooo, just Dos Equis, Sam Adams, Bud, and Miller Lite."

"How about Sierra Nevada?" I'm not kidding, this is still the same guy.

Fed up, Brandon looks over to Logan and yells across to the other side of the bar, "Hey Logan. Do we have Sierra Nevada down there?"

Logan Farrar, knowing the well-rehearsed routine, drops what he's doing, walks over to the tap handles, stares them down like it was his first day as well, and says, "Nooo, looks like all we have is Dos Equis, Sam Adams, Bud, and Miller Lite."

"Nope, I guess that's all we have," Brandon told the oblivious customer. The customer at that point figured that's actually all we had and gave up.

We always joke around about keeping a hidden tap handle in the reach-in cooler out of the sight of customers. However, we have to be careful so no customers believe there *is* one in there.

WHAT THE HELL IS WRONG WITH YOU!?

* * *

Another thing that happens on a daily basis is when someone asks for something that we don't have. Hang on just a second, I know what you're thinking, and I know that there is no way someone could possibly know the entire menu. That isn't what bothers me. What does bug me is when they ask for things that we don't have after I tell them we don't have it. I guess they ask out of disbelief. Then when they finally believe me that we don't have that particular item, they enter into some kind of shock.

"What do ya mean ya'll aint got Coor's!?" This is something I hear far to often. Of course, once again, to the customer it's all my fault that we don't. I promise you, I wasn't the person in the board meeting that said, "You know, let's not carry Coor's, piss some people off." Actually, that does sound like something I would do, but rest assured, it wasn't me.

* * *

Another fun one is when someone walks up to the bar and asks for a Bud Light. I would say, "How about a Bud?"

"What? You don't have Bud Light?"

All right, there are so many things that you could say back to this person. I've used all of the following:

- (*If they had asked me what we had) "Yeah, I just didn't feel like listing it."
- "Yes we do, but you can't have any."
- "Yeah, but I'm really trying to sell the regular Bud first."
- "Does it matter?"

* * *

I just wanted to throw this one in because it makes me just shake my head trying to understand some people. It covers the other aspect of the subject above. When you walk into an establishment, you should have some idea of what type of products that they would serve. It's downright astonishing the things that people have asked me for *at the airport*. I will have to admit, even

WHAT THE HELL IS WRONG WITH YOU!?

though our selection is limited, at least we offer more than Bud and Corona. The following is a list of what people have asked either myself or another employee at the airport bar at one time or another. Keep in mind that everything in this book is real. Now, half of these things listed below you could find in a normal bar, just as long as it's a small dive in North Dakota. The other half of the list is indigenous to your local convenience store. You'll know which is which.

- ✓ Schlitz
- ✓ Pabst Blue Ribbon
- ✓ Milwaukee Light (on tap)
- ✓ Michelob Golden Light
- ✓ Old English
- ✓ Old Style
- ✓ Mickey's Malt Liquor
- ✓ Mad Dog
- ✓ Keystone (in a can)
- ✓ Busch
- ✓ (My personal favorite) Night Train

Don't get the wrong impression; these are all fine products. They just aren't necessarily targeted to marketed airport clientele. I don't know why not, I mean come on, who doesn't like 'kickin' it wit da homies wit a forty of OE while waitin' for my ride from the airport, yo!'

* * *

On the same note, recently, I had a guy walk up to the bar and ask for a beer that I have never heard of before. I wonder why that could be? Check it out:

"Do you have Alaskan?" Working in an airport, my brain immediately thought Alaskan Airlines, and no, we don't *have* Alaskan Airlines, but we do take their meal vouchers if you're delayed long enough and have one for food. So the best logical answer I could come up with was, "What?"

"Alaskan Amber," he said in a tone as if I was going to slap my forehead and reach for my Mentos.

"Nope, I'm afraid not."

"You don't!? It's only the best beer in the world!" he said angrily as he hit his hands on the bar, "what's wrong with you people!? Jeez!"

"I don't know, maybe we don't have it because you are in an airport? In the middle of the desert? How about a Bud?"

I had obviously missed that survey.

* * *

Here's a good way to insult my intelligence! A man walked up to the bar and says, "Ya'll got Keer'z?"

"Nope, sorry buddy, no Coor's products," I replied.

"What? No Keer'z? What kind of bar doesn't have Keer'z?" Obviously showing the expected reaction.

"Not even in bottles?" Again, I'm not kidding. He asked me like I would say, "Oh yeah! That's right! Shoot! Forgot about the bottles."

Continuing on with the same customer, "You know, they don't have Keer'z in Jamaica either, that's kind of funny. All they had was that Red Stripe stuff. I didn't like that," he opinionated, but when you're used to bottled water – just my opinion. I was actually flabbergasted that this person could find himself in Jamaica. What could have drawn him? I guess that's a different story altogether!

* * *

Ah, this one brings me back. This is one of the only times that I became so perturbed; I needed a server to translate for me. This guy walked up to the bar and sits down right in front of the tap handles.

"What can I get for you, brother?" I asked.

What The Hell Is Wrong With You!?

"I'll just have a beer." He replied.

"Okay, what flavor?"

"I don't care which one, just a beer."

"Large draft?" I said holding up the glass like I always do.

"I don't want one of those light beers." Which didn't really answer my question.

"Okay, large draft?" I asked holding the glass up a little higher.

"I'm a light weight, so I want a real beer." He said, not even making sense now.

"Large draft?" I said a little louder while I shook the glass that I would've used in front of his face. Right before I started to hit him with the beer glass before he said another irrelevant statement, Marie, one of the servers stuck her head around the server well to translate.

"I think he wants to know what size beer you want." Marie told the customer with a smile on her face.

"Oh, is that what you're doing," he said as his mind focused, "I just want a beer."

Before we went full circle again, I decided for him. I just gave him a small one because my nerves were pulsating so rapidly at the time, it started to affect the telephone system in the bar.

He did finish with a, "Yeah, there's so many kinds of beers these days."

I didn't respond, I think out of fear.

* * *

I go to that bar called Old Chicago in Tempe, Arizona quite often. My friend Abbie Diersen, who's one of the bartenders, reminded me of another similar situation. When people ask what is on tap when the tap handles are illegible or not visible, I can understand. Hell, I've done the same. But people will actually walk up to this bar; despite the fact that there are twenty-four tap

<u>handles at eye level</u> sticking out of the wall, and ask, "Do you have any beers on tap?"

I feel especially bad for the people that ask that to Abbie. She isn't nearly as lenient as I am. But I still love you, Abbie!

CHAPTER NUMERO SEIS: SKILLS IN TIME MANAGEMENT

Time is a constant, unless you are in a restaurant. For some reason, when someone is waiting in a restaurant for something, time goes by quicker than it does in the rest of the world. It even goes by quicker than your watch, the time on your computers, or any clocks in the restaurant (if applicable) as well. It's really an amazing phenomenon. I think that I actually have discovered the formula to properly figure out *time*. It's pretty easy too. All you have to do is take the actual amount of time that a customer has been waiting, double it, then add five minutes. For all you people who didn't forget algebra like I did, I believe it would be $x=2y+5$. Your solution will be the amount of time that the customer **thinks** they have been waiting. It seems to usually work out. For instance, just say someone has been waiting for five minutes for their drink, they will tell you it's been fifteen. If someone tells you that they've been waiting for their food for forty-five minutes, it's really only been twenty.

Recently I had a table that was ready to go. It was moderately busy in the bar when they gave me their credit card to run through. Along with the other work that I had to do, it took me about 2½ minutes to consolidate my trips and return their credit card slip. It was then when they exclaimed, "Where have you been? We were just going to leave! It's been like ten minutes and we haven't seen you! We need to go!"

They were obviously using the formula. What I wanted to do at that moment was to scold them. Have them sit down – put

What The Hell Is Wrong With You!?

them in a 'time out' if you will, just so I could disappear in back to **show them** what ten minutes *really* feels like!

* * *

I remember in a few places that I've worked at before; we would get incredibly busy for lunch. Ticket times would be up to forty-five minutes. That's right people. Use the formula. Those poor bastards really thought, and had told me, that they had waited an hour and a half!! (I doubt they were even hungry anymore). And, of course you know, once again it's all my fault so I don't get a tip. I guess they figured I was in the kitchen physically holding the cook's arms back chanting, "Don't cook that! Don't cook that!"

I guess I deserve not getting a tip in that situation. I mean, I guess I could have gone to the kitchen, kicked out all the cooks, thrown away everyone else's tickets, and just made <u>my</u> tables food to show good service. Well, maybe not because then they would just bitch about not having their drinks refilled while I cooked their food. Those bastards. I mean, poor bastards. No, I mean bastards.

Airport Time?

I'm not sure how or where this started, but someone must have started a rumor years and years ago that airports have different times than the city you are in. I know that doesn't make too much sense. It's like an, 'airport time', if you will. One of the servers at the airport bar, Becca Brassard, was one of the first people to bring this to my attention.

"Excuse me, do you know what the local time is?" The traveler asked.

"Sure, it's 7:34," Becca replied.

"No, I mean the airport time." I rest my case. Really, does that make sense to anyone!?

WHAT THE HELL IS WRONG WITH YOU!?

You know, twice a year, the airline industry goes nuts when people miss flights all over the country due to the seasonal time changes. We're actually pretty lucky here in Arizona because we never need to change our clocks around. Of course, in turn, it screws up everybody else that has a layover in Phoenix. The point that I'm trying to get to is this: Could you imagine if there was such a thing as 'airport time'? Nobody would ever catch his or her flights! If you were a business traveler, you would need a whole bunch of watches; one for every city you would stop in **and** their respective 'airport times'. Which makes me wonder, would the 'airport time' be the same at all of the airports, or would each airport have it's own 'airport time'? You know, it's hurting my head to think about it, I'm going to have to change the subject before my head explodes. You may feel free to draw your own conclusions.

* * *

Another quick story about time happened to me recently. Unfortunately, I always think of the perfect thing to say when it's too late. This guy walks up to the bar and asks what time it is. I tell him it's 2:45. He then said one of the smartest things you could possibly ask someone wearing a watch.

"So, is that time pretty accurate?"

Hmm. I guess it's feasible that, working at the airport, I would have the *inaccurate* time so people would miss their flights and get pissed off (or more pissed off) at me. That would really make my job more bearable. Hell, I could just make up times. There aren't any clocks in the bar – why not? That's what I should have said. Midnight. It's always midnight.

* * *

This one happened to me just a couple of days ago. It was so good and stupid that I had to tack it on. I had a gentleman at the bar ARGUING with me about what time it was. Why the fuck did you ask!? I guess he didn't realize that he was traveling across

What The Hell Is Wrong With You!?

different time zones and the time on my watch was from where *I live.* Duh. I guess I could start confusing the half-normal people. They'd ask me what time it is and I could say, "Well, that all depends. Where you from? Oh, it's midnight."

If You're In A Hurry, Don't Sit Down

Even though we serve fast food at the bar in the airport, when we have about 400 people in the bar and another 30 or so next door getting food from the same kitchen, it could take a while for food. This is especially true seeing that the people standing at a counter will be served first. The people sitting down will be served later, because they are sitting down, get it? For the most part, if you go to a restaurant and sit down and every employee you see is just freaking out, and the pass through window has food piled on top of food itself, and there are still people coming in; it will, not might, <u>will</u> take a while for food. It's so disconcerting how people can enter this situation, sit down, and get pissed off because they can't get a burrito in two and a half minutes. It's even more frustrating to know that they can, they just have to go next door!

Becca told me another story about customers misunderstanding the concepts of time when it comes to getting food. It also shows that I'm not the only one who gets fed up.

"How long does the food take?" A customer queried.

"Everything on the menu takes at least fifteen minutes when we are busy." Becca replied. (Even thought the customer should be thinking thirty-five minutes, if he knows the formula.)

"Chips and salsa takes fifteen minutes?" He asked in disbelief.

"Chips and salsa would be included in 'everything'." Retorted Becca.

What The Hell Is Wrong With You!?

I'm Special ~ I Have A Plane To Catch

One of everyone's all time favorite things to hear from a customer at the airport is that they are in a hurry because they have a plane to catch. This phrase is used so often, it just makes us laugh at you now. I guess these customers figured that we're just a normal bar with a bad location and really crappy parking. So everyone knows, we've all figured it out. We know that you are all eating or drinking at the airport because of something to do with an airplane.

There was this one time when I was serving that I (once again) reached my breaking point. I was starting to get very busy when an older woman dressed in business attire came in, sat down at my table, and said without the respect of looking up at me, "I would like a chicken burrito, a margarita, and you put a hurry on it, I have a plane to catch."

Instantly upset, I didn't bother asking her if she wanted a double shot, rocks or frozen, salted rim, I just didn't care. I guess that's what ten years will do to you. Soon after ringing up her food, I ran over to the pass through window, and just to make others around me laugh, I yelled, "Hey, I just rang in an order for a chicken burrito, yeah, that's right, among the other twelve, but this lady in my section needs hers first because she has a plane to catch!!"

All of the servers started laughing, because they hear it all the time. What I didn't notice right away is that all the customers that heard me were laughing as well. Unfortunately, the lady who ordered it didn't hear me. Too bad.

One of these days, though, I will lose it completely. Actually, a couple other employees that I work with have the same prophesy about this situation. One of these times, probably soon, someone is going to go to the bar and say they are in a hurry and have a plane to catch. Whoever snaps first will ask the person's

WHAT THE HELL IS WRONG WITH YOU!?

name, we'll say it's Bob. His name will be the last thing that he will say because of sheer embarrassment. In the best possible ringleader voice, an announcement will be made.

"Ladies and gentlemen, may I have your attention please! Sitting directly in front of me at the end of the bar is Bob! Bob is much more important than any of you! He, has a plane to catch! Per the request of Bob, all of your drink and food orders will be on hold until Bob gets his first! I apologize for the delay. Just be thankful that you don't have a plane to catch here *at the airport*! Thank you!"

This day will live in infamy.

What The Hell Is Wrong With You!?

I'm Your Bartender, Not Your Babysitter

This one only happens at the airport. These are a few other episodes that happen on a frequent basis when travelers get upset with me, the bartender, because I 'made them' miss their flight. I wonder if these people actually think that I have the mental ability, or the baby-sitting skills, to find out and remember everybody's itinerary. You know, if I could do that, I sure as shit wouldn't be a bartender. If you think about it, there's about 30 flights in my shift, with an average of 125 people a flight, if half of those people come in and out of the bar, well, hell, that's only 1,875 people that I would need to keep track of. Not a problem, I love a good challenge.

I also love the people that think that the company I work for, 'OCD roast', is in cahoots with the airlines and that's why flights get delayed. So people will go to the bars. I would like to say that that's the most ridiculous think I have ever heard, but unfortunately, I can't. The worst part about these bitter people that believe that, of course, take it out on me. Once again, it's all my fault that your flight got delayed. I didn't think you were able to see me on the tarmac with my wine opener slashing airplane tires, come on people! So, seeing that it's my company's fault, and my fault, the grumpy drinker will pay with exact change, leave me no tip, and give me a dirty look. Hey, thank God I don't live off tips...wait a minute, shit! I do! I'll get more into that in chapter eleven.

What The Hell Is Wrong With You!?

Did You Make It By Close? Good For You!

This one I had to put in at the last minute because of the importance of this situation that happens normally. This one comes to you from any given restaurant or any given bar. It has to do with people that come in right before, or right at 'closing time'.

I need to point out that this deals more so with the restaurant aspect than it does the bar aspect. If you get off of work and can make it to your frequented bar or pub for last call, this is good. And good for you – sometimes I am not as lucky. The scenario that I want to bring up deals with working in a restaurant or a bar that serves food. This is here to explain what happens in an establishment that closes at eleven o'clock, and people walk in at 10:53. I put this extra section in to enlighten those who don't know, and sympathize with those who do, how horrible this atrocity is.

People who have never worked in a restaurant before will not know this ahead of time, but believe me, it's fact. The last (at least) half an hour before the scheduled closing time of any restaurant or bar is dedicated to closing and cleaning. I know that many will and have a problem with this, but it's a normality with many a restaurant worker across America. No one waits until they are closed to begin cleaning. No one. Let me run down what actually happens when one of these latecomers comes into play.

This will usually happen, due to Murphy's Law, when you are caught up with most of your closing duties to leave either on the time that you planned, or maybe even early. You will be closing down whatever you need to, and you will see *them*. These people, sometimes but rarely innocently, will wander in just a couple minutes before the doors **need** to be locked. Due to the way that restaurants work, these people <u>will be served</u>. These people will also see certain signs from the server (and/or other employees including management) to try to hint to the fact that the restaurant has closed and that people want to leave. For instance, everyone employed will look at his or her watches, or a nearby clock when at the table. Rest assured, they know what time it is. I actually had a manager vociferously exclaim to me in my station, "The kitchen is closed; do you have anymore orders?" – when he knew I didn't.

Sometimes I wish it were like the DMV (or DOT, dependent on where you are); when they close, they tell all the people which who are still in line – to leave. Then the common folk have no choice.

This should give you a good idea of the chain reaction caused by last minute diners. A lot of people think that servers and restaurant workers don't want to wait on them because they are just lazy. This is further from the truth. Restaurant workers are usually very efficient, especially when it comes to cleaning. When a last minute table comes in, they stand in the way of efficiency. Half the things that have been cleaned up will be dirtied again; and in turn, will need to be cleaned again. This is just the tip of the iceberg.

When late drinks are ordered, by then all the ice has been burnt (melted). The server or bartender will have to make an extra trip to get ice from in back. The server or bartender will also have to take out anything that was put away like salad dressings, salad, salsa, chips, bread, anything dairy, etc. The employees will also have to restock everything used back to capacity. Extra trips mean extra time.

When the server or bartender is back there, they will inform the kitchen that there is another table. The crew in the kitchen will become outraged because cleaning a kitchen is much more difficult than one would think. Now the person in the kitchen yells at the servers or bartenders like it's their fault. I remember when I was a cook; the server was the only person I could vent on.

WHAT THE HELL IS WRONG WITH YOU!?

When the guests at the table receive their food, the kitchen begins to clean up any mess that was made, wasting their time. The dishwasher in the back, who at this time is completely done, has to stay longer to wash your dishes. Now it becomes a labor issue. The restaurant will need to pay for the extra wages to sit and watch you eat.

By the time that the last minute table is finishing up, the server or bartender will be sitting in a nearby table, about 30 to 45 minutes beyond normal waiting for you to pay your tab. The server or bartender will not be able to do his or her paperwork until all the tables have closed out. Then after doing the paperwork, the server or bartender will have to clean up after the latecomers. To top it all off, the manager will have to stay that much longer because he or she won't be able to start any end-of-the-day paperwork until all the tables have closed out.

So now time has been taken out of at least four people's lives so you can eat at that particular restaurant. It's heartbreaking to think that going to a twenty-four hour establishment is just too much when you eat dinner at almost eleven at night.

I have wished for one of these last minute tables to do this: Knowing we were closed and having the audacity to ask me for dessert when they were done. I would have no choice but to tell them the truth. "The cook had already gone home for the day."

The most important point is this: When you come into a restaurant at the last minute, you lengthen the working time of almost everyone there. Some could say that it's extra money, but usually, it's not; it's just extra time wasted. Many, many restaurant workers have families and other obligations to attend to – even that late at night. I personally get a feeling of inconsideration when people do this, but I have to remember it's because people probably don't understand. I guess that's why I'm writing this.

WHAT THE HELL IS WRONG WITH YOU!?

DON'T GET YOUR DRINKS AT THE BAR AND THEN DIRTY MY TABLE ~ SHITHEAD

I needed to save this one for the last because I wasn't really sure which chapter to put it in. I guess it applies to time because whenever I catch someone doing this, they always say something about time. Either I took to long, or they didn't have time to wait, or I'm an incredible idiot; what have you.

This is a really good example of where my anger level can take me. The strange time thing and the rudeness and blatant lying ability of the common confronted customer don't bother me nearly as much as a different pet peeve. This is by far my worst pet peeve when I'm serving tables. That peeve is when a customer goes to the bar, buys drinks from the bartender, then sits at one of my tables. In some cases it can be acceptable in my mind. For instance, when I'm slammed and can't get to every table in my station because we're short staffed, or if you're in a really small bar like a hotel lounge that doesn't have servers. I actually had to tell my managers at the airport that I needed to lose my serving shifts and just bartend, or I would have to find a new job. That's how pissed off I get. I do know that it's partially my fault, because other servers get upset and then blow it off. I can't blow it off; I usually just blow up.

I'll break it down for you so you can understand why I get so pissed. Mr. X goes to the bar, orders his drink, tips the bartender, and then sits at my table. Usually, because I don't bring cocktail napkins because I don't even want to talk to the likes of Mr. X, he will leave a mess on the table. When he leaves, I get to clean up the mess for two dollars an hour and no tip. Here's where it gets really frustrating; at the end of the night, I get to tip the bartender, again. It's very upsetting to me because there is no one I can really technically get mad at. The customer is an idiot and never gives me a chance to do my job as a server, the bartender is

WHAT THE HELL IS WRONG WITH YOU!?

just doing his or her job, and I can't blame the kitchen (a little joke for you cooks out there). Regardless, there have been nights where this would happen four or five times in a row filling half of my section. So I don't make any money at all, but I do get to clean up after everyone. This instantly turns me into an underpaid, glorified busboy. That's usually when you can find me in the walk-in beating the shit out of a box of diced onions. Hey, it's either that or someone's head. I'm looking out.

Now that you know what really pisses me off, I can tell you this story. We will use Mr. X. Mr. X and his wife, Mrs. X, came in and sat at one of my tables. Mr. X started to head towards the door as I walked up to the table. I figured that he was going to the bathroom, or something. I would say that they did actually both sit down for about thirty seconds before I arrived at the table. I then asked Mrs. X if I could get them something to drink.

"Oh, I'm sorry, my husband already went to the bar." She replied. I turned around and sure as shit, there he was. I lividly bee-lined it up to the bar to intercept. This is one of the only things that I can do to calm my already troubled nerves.

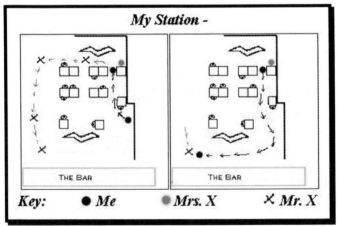

"Are you guys sitting back at that table?" I asked politely.

78

WHAT THE HELL IS WRONG WITH YOU!?

"Yeah," his return seemed a little cocky.

Still remaining calm, I told him, "Well, for future reference, we have table service and I can help you back there."

Cutting me off, this jackass, I mean Mr. X said, "Well, for *your* future reference we were sitting back there for ten minutes!"

"That's BULLSHIT!" I had snapped, "I just cleaned that table no more then two minutes ago!" I even had the paperwork in the computer to prove it. He had no response, returned to his table and sat down. Every time I walked by their table, he would stare me down. I replied with a very authoritative and loud, "Is everything okay here." (Notice, it's not a question at this point.) Later, I did actually, by Mr. X's request, served them and they did tip me pretty well. It was probably out of fear of what I would have done if he didn't.

The moral of this story: Restaurant workers can have the attitude of Mary Poppins until you fuck up and say or do something stupid, and then out comes Godzilla. Always, be cautious because you never know when one of us is about to snap.

What The Hell Is Wrong With You!?

Chapter Numero Siete: A Menu Is A Listing Of What Is Served. How Hard Is This?

I know that I had brought this up before, but I need to say it again. Be thankful that I don't say these things nearly as often as I hear them. After staring at the menu of Mexican food for a few minutes, people will start asking if we have other, I guess, secret items that we figured we wouldn't list. After looking at the menu, people will ask for hot dogs, French fries, hamburgers, hot wings, salads, sandwiches, snacks, bags of chips, candy bars, sushi, etc. One of the servers that works there, Ralph, likes his retort the best. When he greets one of his tables, they will instantly ask something like, "Don't you have any salads?"

"That's our entire menu," Ralph will tell them.

"Well, how about French fries?" They will ask because they got lost on the word 'entire'.

"That's our entire menu," Ralph would say again with a little more agitation. I've worked with Ralph long enough to know that until those people order something off the menu, or leave, he will keep saying, "That's our entire menu," over and over again. With each time he says this, he will throw in a 'fucking' or two in for emphasis. This is also the guy that if you, his customer, snap or whistle to get his attention, he will drop what he's doing and say something like, "You snap at me one more fucking time and, so help me God, I will punch you in the face!"

At least he's not angry when he says it, really. He just merely states a fact. Not to mention, he's getting it out right away before it turns into pent up aggression.

* * *

By the way, here you go Ralph: Ralph also wanted me to mention that 'he's the coolest mother fucker that you could ever have the pleasure to know.' At this time, he's probably flying jets

WHAT THE HELL IS WRONG WITH YOU!?

for the Navy in Florida protecting the freedom and rights of the American people for reasons of patriotism and honor...just like in *Top Gun* (That's right, I *am* dangerous!). I hope that about covered it for you Ralph.

* * *

One of the things I love about working at the airport is that you meet such a diverse group of people. It's really too bad how it opens your eyes to the less intelligent half of them.

Our menu is pretty simple, it's all Mexican food and it's all on one page. I don't know how it happens or where some of these people come from, but never in my life, until I worked at the airport, was I ever asked to describe a taco. Nor tell someone what a burrito is. I know that I'm in Arizona, and here, burritos are second nature, but I haven't been here all of my life. I have lived and traveled to many, many states and have seen many, many things. I've been in Florida, through the south, Kansas, the Dakotas, the Midwest, and the west coast. No matter where I have gone, I have seen lots of pretty women and TACO BELLS. I really would like to know if these people that don't know what a taco is (usually pronounced 'take-oh') think when they drive by a Taco Bell. They probably think, "Do we need any bells? Nope. I wonder how that take-oh guy does just selling bells." I couldn't possibly fathom what could be thought in the vicinity of a Del Taco.

WHAT THE HELL IS WRONG WITH YOU!?

SO YOU SAY YOU'RE READY TO ORDER, HUH?

This is one that anyone who has worked in the restaurant industry can relate with. I don't understand why people do this. I actually have a theory that maybe they didn't get the parental attention as children so psychologically they have to find it somewhere else. Does that mean that these people are messed up? No, not really, but what they do is pretty messed up. When I walk up to a table or a customer at the bar, I'll ask them a simple, closed answer question:

"Hey, have you decided what you want?"

Simple questions deserve simple answers. If the answer is no, that's okay, I'll come back, soon, honest, I promise. Please, for the love of all that is holy, don't say 'yes' and then continue to decide. This is the most blatant waste of time out of just about anything else I can think of. It's like you attach a shackle to my ankle and the base of your table! It's rude if I just walk away, so of course, as I look around at all the other people I could be serving, I say one of these lines:

"Do you need another minute?"

"I'll be right back."

"Haven't decided yet? That's okay, I can come back."

These are usually followed with a verbal negative gesture like 'nooahhaha' and sometimes, unwarranted physical contact like grabbing my arm or the towel hanging from my belt (I hate that!). So with the shackles still in place, I wait while you read the entire menu. Time is money and you are stupid.

I have actually gotten to the point where I will just walk away now without saying anything. It usually hurts my tip, I'm sure, but it makes me feel so much better! What would really make me feel better is if people didn't do this. If you don't know what you want to eat, you can't tell me. In turn I can't tell the

What The Hell Is Wrong With You!?

kitchen. If you're not part of the solution…stop being part of the problem!

You Must Really Be Hungry

Becca comes to me with another story from the airport that instantly noted its way onto a cocktail napkin for this book. With all the burritos that we serve, you have a choice whether your burrito will be made with steak or chicken. Becca had a table that ordered some burritos. As you could probably figure out, she asked them if they wanted steak or chicken. They all said steak. When the table received their food, they all looked puzzled as they examined their plates. They seemed to be thinking whether or not they received the right thing. Becca, picking up on this, asked if everything was okay. They said, "Well, we have our burritos, but where's our steaks?"

They actually expected, along with this strange, but very large burrito, to receive a steak on the side, From a Mexican fast-food joint in the airport. That's just wrong for so many reasons. Thank you Becca.

What Kind Of Restaurant Only Has One Menu?

Another daily thing that is asked to each and every one of us is this: When someone is looking at the menu, they will get your attention and ask you, "Is this your only menu?"

Before I list what we do to people like this, I would like you to close your eyes and think of how many restaurants you have been to that have had two menus, but will only give you one. It's never happened to me. It's just bad marketing! A point to remember when you are reading this list is that none of this is made up. All of these things have been done in response.

What The Hell Is Wrong With You!?

Question: "Is this your only menu?"
Answers:
- "No, we have another menu in the back for the smart people."
- "No, here you go." (Handing them another copy of the same menu)
- "Why, is that one broken?"
- "Yeah, we have another one, but you can't have any of *that* food."

Most of these responses have come from my friend Rae Rae. She feels the same daily rage as I.

It's Okay To Be 'Uni-Lingual'

The last thing about the menus is this: If you go to a Mexican restaurant, or any other restaurant of a different origin than your own, and you can't pronounce the words on the menu, don't. It's much better for you just to point the item out than trying to pronounce it. Not only will it be quicker to order because the server doesn't have to wait while you stutter through the word 'fajita', but it will save yourself a little face. Also, don't make up fake menu names unless it's a joke AND it's funny. If it doesn't fit <u>both</u> of these categories, keep it to yourself.

In case you do this, this will help you a great deal: In Spanish, the group of letters 'que' is pronounced as a 'k'. For instance, how you would say 'what' in Spanish. 'Queso' is cheese. You will find 'queso' in many Mexican dishes. Please stop calling it 'Kweso'. Two 'l's next to each other (ll) makes a 'y' sound. When you ask for chicken in Spanish, pollo, it's pronounced 'poi-yo'. Polo is a game with big hammers and horses. I think we are

WHAT THE HELL IS WRONG WITH YOU!?

all familiar with the word 'tortilla'. If you must pronounce these words, please use caution; improper diction causes mild aneurisms.

As found in many Mexican restaurants around the country, one of the items we serve is called the 'Ultimate Margarita'. I was actually asked more than once for a 'Margarita Ultimo'. Granted, I understood even though it means 'last margarita'. I couldn't stop laughing because I instantly pictured this:

WHAT THE HELL IS WRONG WITH YOU!?

Just as the fate of St.Pueblo, a small village in the heart of Mexico, was being plagued with the problem of no lime refreshment, all the villagers fret. Just when everything looked it's bleakest and nothing else could save them from this vicious wrath, they know what they needed. They needed a hero, a savior. One that would come with a plentiful amount of that concoction that helps them hang on. 'Look, there, up in the sky! It's a piñata! It's a burrito! NO, it's...Margarita Ultimo!!

'Dejale todo a mi!! Yo tengo bastante pa' todos!'
-Margarita Ultimo

Whew, that was fun, thank you.

WHAT THE HELL IS WRONG WITH YOU!?

CHAPTER NUMERO OCHO: DEALING WITH TELEVISIONS AND AUDIO SYSTEMS

Who out there likes to watch TV when you're at a bar? What's that? Everyone? Okay, cool. This chapter has so many attributes, I'm not really sure where to start. When I worked at McDuffy's, they had, and still have over seventy televisions. Now when you're in a big sports bar like that, and you want to watch *women's underwater basket weaving*, you might get lucky. At the airport, on the other hand, you will not have that luxury. I really wanted to start with this. One of my favorite things that people say when they want a television changed is, "Well, nobody's watching that anyway!"

What an amazing ability that some customers think they have! Knowing that, in a room having up to one to two hundred people behind him, not one person is watching the game that's on the television he or she wants changed.

A good example of this happened to me just a few days ago. I was at work and we just went through a little rush. There was still quite a few people in the bar area, but they were just hanging out at that point. I was washing glassware talking to the leftover few people at the bar and watching the Arizona Diamondbacks playing baseball. It was 3:27pm Phoenix time (or midnight, airport time); the score was Arizona 7, Colorado 7. It was top of the 10th inning in overtime and this woman at the bar says, "Nobody's watching this, could you turn it to the Braves?"

First of all, you're in Arizona. No, we are watching it you idiot! Secondly, the Braves? Come on! I could just take a good guess at whose winning and probably be right. No offence.

Another example is here: Once, I changed all the TV's around in McDuffy's at the request of a bunch of customers. They were all lined up at the skybox, the area with all the A/V equipment. One by one, they all told me which games to put where. After being scolded by my boss, Jake Guzman, I got yelled at by pretty much every other patron that was not at the skybox. The lesson that I learned was not to ever touch the TVs, ever. Actually, I've modified that rule after I left McDuffy's. The rule that the bartenders at the airport follow is this: The TVs stay on whatever the bartenders put it on. Fuck off.

What I don't understand is that when a customer wants a channel changed, that's all they can care about. At the airport, I can get real damn busy. All it takes is two flights to be delayed at the same time, which happens quite often, and we'll have 300 new people in the bar. Consequently, we'll have 300 drinks for the two bartenders to make, all at once. At any given time, I could be working behind the fifteen-seat bar at the airport, that will be two or three people deep waiting to order, and server drink orders coming off the printer and trailing down four feet to the floor. People will come up to me and say, "Hey, could you change the TV to the Nascar race?"

Even though, I making drinks so fast that I can't even look up at this person to respond, they feel the need to ask me over and over, getting louder each time, until I do respond.

"No." Is usually my response; especially if there's a hockey game on. Hell, he might as well say, "Could you drop what you're doing and search the DSS system for something that you probably won't find anyway to piss off everybody else in the bar waiting for their drinks so I can watch the cars racing? Obviously, I'm the only one here."

FORE! LOOKOUT ~ IDIOT

While I'm on the subject of televisions, I'll tell you a little tale of the golf fan that knew too little. I was working a day shift with Martinez, another bartender who usually takes care of the TVs. He follows all sports, while I just follow hockey and dabble here and there with the others. The Masters were coming on at two o'clock. I know this for a fact because everybody, and their dog, asked us up until it started what time it began. It was about ten minutes after one o'clock when this older guy starts freaking out because we didn't have the Masters on TV. He first yelled at his server. That server asked me about it and I said it didn't start until two. He argued that it started at one; he saw it on television that morning. I guess he didn't figure on that whole silly 'time zone' thing from before. When he finished arguing with his server, he walked up to the bar and yelled at me. I told him that I couldn't change it until two and that I was sorry. He got a little more upset and went to Martinez. Not unlike Abbie at Old Chicago, Martinez is also not as forgiving as myself. The old guy told him the same story about how it started at one. Martinez told him to go sit down and it will be on when it starts. That wasn't good enough, the old guy persisted with the added threat, "Do you want me to cancel my order?"

A little side note here; don't ever threaten like that. Your answer will either be, "Please do, because we really don't need your bitch ass in here, okay?" Or, "I'm sorry, but I don't give a hairy rat's ass."

Now that Martinez was upset, he grabbed the sports page from the newspaper, opened it to the *Today's Broadcasts* section, folded it like a road map and presented it to the old man. The old guy didn't take the paper because he now knew that he was wrong, but still fought the futile battle.

"Your newspaper's wrong so just change it!" That was the last thing that he said. Frustrated, Martinez dropped what he was doing to briefly change one of the DSS systems to the channel that would hold the Masters only to find a blank screen. The old guy already sat back down at his table, but Martinez still turned around to say, "See, I told you it isn't on until two, stupid!"

What The Hell Is Wrong With You!?

I still don't understand what he could have missed if it had already started. Don't get me wrong, I've watched a little golf before, and at times I have found it interesting. One of the most interesting things I've ever seen on an open was a putt made by Tiger Woods. He shot this putt that went five feet up to the right and then rolled back down another five feet to the left and into the hole. I certainly wouldn't be able to do it. Then he held his putter in his left hand while doing this pumping motion with his right. Everybody was cheering and the announcers were going nuts. They said, "Whoa, that was great, let's look at that again!" Now, when they said that, I thought that they were going to show a replay of the putt, but they didn't. Instead, they showed Tiger's celebration of the 'cha-ching' style body movements. Then they showed his celebration again. Then once again from the reverse angle. Not once did they show the putt again. I have never understood that.

Maybe that's what the old guy was afraid of missing. I can't see why, it would have been on the highlight reel, right?

Why Did You Even Ask Me To Change It?

Please be cautious not to do this: Every once in a while a guy will come in and sit down at the bar and bitch every two minutes for you to change the television channel while you're busy as hell. This has all been explained in detail before.

As a lot of people know, bartenders, like children and animals, have selective hearing. If we don't want to hear you, we just flip off the little switch in our heads (and probably flip you off as well).

Taking in account the two points here, the worst part is this: After not asking, but bitching numerous times in the past ten minutes while we are really busy assisting other customers, we do change the big screen to the channel of your choosing. Then you

What The Hell Is Wrong With You!?

bury your head in a newspaper and don't even look up! Yes, we have watched you, and we are always watching you.

Music Is Part Of The 'Bar Ambiance'

The other aspect of this chapter is audio equipment. Just so you know, if you go into a bar, the music will probably be a little on the loud side. It certainly will not be background music. If this is too much for you to handle, DON'T GO TO A BAR!! Go to the library, or a coffee house, or better yet, just stay at home. If the music does get too loud, we will notice and fix it. Usually, if it's too loud, it's due to a song or CD changing that has a different recording level. I do have to tell the whole truth and say that, yes; at times I have had the music real loud because it's hard to hear the music from behind the bar. The servers usually adjust it before a customer asks me to turn it down. All the other times that customers have asked me to turn it down, it has always been at an acceptable level. Acceptable for a bar.

This particular bitch is a serious one for bar employees, especially when it's busy. When you work in a bar, the only form of entertainment available for us when we're busy, besides bar tricks, is the music. Asking us to turn it down is like going into a TGI Friday's and saying, "If you wouldn't mind, could you stop tossing those bottles around like that?" You just don't do that, you know?

What The Hell Is Wrong With You!?

Chapter Numero Nueve: A Particular Breed Of Motor Sport Fan And Everything Else That Is Classy

Just to start, I would like to say that there is nothing wrong with motor sports. I'm personally not a big fan. I never got into it, can't really see the sport. There were a few parts of *Days Of Thunder* that I did like, the stripper, the storyline, the drama, and the stripper. That's my opinion. You know what they say about opinions, they're like assholes, everyone has one and it usually stinks (unless your 'shit don't stink'). Even with my opinion, I have a lot of friends that are heavily into motor sports. These are not the people that I am talking about. I am talking about a different breed. A special percentage of motor sport fans are certainly unique. The best way that I've heard it put from a customer was 'Jerry Springer Guests'.

Now if you like motor sports, and do not follow the following description, I'm not talking about you. You are fine. I can't stress this enough.

Without getting too brutal, I'll just point out a couple of traits that this percentage does on a normal basis. And then I will tell you a few stories of what these people have done. For the examples we will call this person Joe-Bob. Joe-Bob will come into *any* bar and do these things, but we will keep it real and use my bar as the example. Joe-Bob will first order something like Old Milwaukee, or Miller Genuine Draft (because it's a sponsor), or other things that we don't have. He will say some comment about how we 'suck' for not having them, then get a different domestic beer, but bitch about it. Joe-Bob, however, would never have anything that's not domestic. He will usually start a tab and never ask how much anything is. Joe-Bob will drink his beer faster than the brewery can produce it. After a few quick beers, Joe-Bob will ask for his tab. We'll say he had four large beers. At the airport, it would be $20.61. First, Joe-Bob will bitch about the prices and ask for something to be done about it. Then, when he realizes that there's nothing we can do about the prices, he will revert to some kind of quantity discount.

"I bought four beers, can't I get one of them for free?"

No, you can't 'buy three - get one free'. Upset that you will not give him free things, like it would matter tip wise, he reluctantly gives you a twenty and a one-dollar bill. Usually, when they do this, they will run for the door before you can say anything about the 39-cent tip, showing that they know they are doing something wrong. Or, they will think that they are saving the whales and say something like, "Hey, keep the change!" Showing that they are just dolts.

Everything above applies IF they aren't first refused service because they are already plowed! I had a customer at the airport after a motor sport race in town that looked like he had been drinking domestic beer for the past 14 hours. He couldn't talk, he could barely walk, and his face looked like a sun-dried tomato. I wasn't going to serve him anything. His friend complained to the manager, because he couldn't speak, and the manager agreed not to serve him, but didn't kick them out. I was given the joy of having them talk shit every time I walked close to them. Well, actually, mumble shit.

I do feel the need to say that the most annoying trait to us is when they don't tip. They never tip. Everything else could be bearable if it wasn't a prelude to the loss of personal income. Tipping is why we serve you. I will tell you all about this in chapter eleven.

Working at the airport, you run into Joe-Bob quite a bit when there is a race in town. Lucky for us, we have two racetracks, and live in a climate that offers year around racing. If you are a 'Joe-Bob', you should definitely pay attention. We always refer to a week of work when all the 'Joe-Bobs' are in town

WHAT THE HELL IS WRONG WITH YOU!?

as 'Nascar week'. This is not a good title for you. It basically translates to: we will be really, really busy and make no money at all. Again, it's all about etiquette. And now for the real stories:

KEEP THE CHANGE? ARE YOU SERIOUS?

In the midst of Nascar week, I was serving in one of the better stations, yet, making no money. No big shocker. Almost every table was like a Joe-Bob and family. One of the things that we are allowed to tell customers is that if they want to be in the bar to smoke, they will have to buy something. Sometimes they just get upset and leave; other times, they will buy a soda or a bottle of water to share amongst three or four people.

Case in point, I had three people take up one of my tables to smoke. They seemed younger so I carded them right away. They were all over twenty-one; so you know – I'm not dealing with some punk kids. They ordered a bottle of water to split. They smoked cigarettes for about twenty-minutes while I made no money off of the table. In that twenty-minute time period, a woman sat down next to them and ordered a soda. I told her that her total was $2.46. The woman drank her soda, smoked her cigarette and left three one-dollar bills when she left. Like I said before, Nascar week is very busy. I saw the three dollars on the table when she left, and was going to pick it up after I took care of a couple of other tables. I never fathomed anyone could do what I'm about to tell you. In passing, the three people asked how much they owed. I told them $2.57. I also noticed that the girl in the group had a handful of change. Every ten or twenty seconds, I would pass buy to see their progress. They counted out their change and seemed to be short. So they took one of the three dollars left by the woman that was next to them, used it to pay for the bottle of water, AND TOOK THE REST OF THE CHANGE!!

WHAT THE HELL IS WRONG WITH YOU!?

That's right. Not only did I lose the 54-cent tip from the soda, but <u>lost</u> 46-cents on that transaction, only to just get stiffed on the bottle of water. I guess I shouldn't really bitch, they did leave a complementary map showing how to get to Phoenix International Raceway from the airport. Hey, that's great, thanks.

IS THAT MY HEAD IN THE NOOSE?

Another wonderful Nascar week story is mysteriously similar. I was really busy and making no money. Funny. Three (different) people sat down at one of my tables to smoke. Upset that they would have to buy something, they ordered a few beers. Then they ordered another round. When they needed to leave, they paid me personally with exact change, to the penny. This has happened to me before where the customers will leave a tip on the table when they get up, so I didn't get angry...at first. After they left, I went to go clean the table to see what they had left me. In place of a tip, I received this: It seems they were playing hangman on a napkin. That's what they left me. An old game of hangman. The funniest part of the story is that the answer to their hangman game was 'Monster Truck Rally'. Except 'rally' was really spelled 'ral<u>ley</u>'. Makes the game more difficult when the secret words are misspelled.

WHAT THE HELL IS WRONG WITH YOU!?

FANS OF MASOCHISM

Again, this is not a rip on motor sports; it is on only some of its fans. Within the percentage that I was talking about before, there lies yet another percentage of a different kind of motor sport fan. Have I lost you Joe-Bob? There are the people that will bitch at you to change the televisions (all of the televisions) to the car race. Once we get the chance to change the TV's around, they usually give cocky thanks as if to say, "What the hell took you so long?"

These same people **will not even watch the race until there is a crash.** Matter of fact, even though they are wearing jackets and hats with different racecar drivers' names and logos on them, I think all they care about are the crashes. There is no sport in crashing, unless it's demolition derbies, but then, why watch motor sports? "Need to Always See Carcasses Across the Road," I'd bet is what these people think.

I do have to admit, crashes in auto racing are the same as fist fights in hockey. It happens, it *is* part of the sport. However, this should not be the reason you watch. Because I am a huge hockey fan, I look at it this way: When I go to a Phoenix Coyotes game, and no fights break out, I still enjoy the game. I have talked to people that have told me that they are disappointed to not see a crash when they watch a race. These are the people you should watch out for on the road, I think.

What The Hell Is Wrong With You!?

Don't They Sell Glassware...Everywhere?

Another thing that I cannot understand with these people in particular is their insatiable want for glassware. This happens with many different sorts of people, but the majority of people that do this are people like Joe-Bob. Everyone asks if we sell shot glasses or other merchandise with our logo on it. We really should, but we don't have any merchandise like that. It's probably a better thing that we don't because, at the airport, a simple T-shirt would probably cost about $200!

Now, I'm not talking about this kind of souvenir glassware. I'm talking about the plain, undecorated, un-etched, regular, everyday, run of the mill, bottom of the barrel pint or pilsner glasses that we put beer in. I'm always flabbergasted when someone asks if they can take them home. I don't understand why. You could literally go to a second hand store and find the same exact crap for like a dollar.

The martini glasses are another favorite amongst the avid bar glass collector. I guess they especially like ours because the stem of the glass is in the shape of a 'z'. They are pretty cool, but once again, found at your local good will. Or, God forbid you would actually have to pay retail, they can be found in any department store.

What makes this so funny is that after these people ask me if they can take the glasses with them, and I say no because they're our glasses (!?), **they take them anyway!** How proud can you possibly be sitting on an airplane on your way home thinking, hey, yeah, I got that pint glass right here in my bag! Or better yet, Joe-Bob has a girl over at his place and says, "Hey baby, you like the glasses? Yep, I snagged 'em from some red headed kid at the airport. Pretty cool, huh."

WHAT THE HELL IS WRONG WITH YOU!?

I remember when I was younger my older sister would have people over at the house. If these people brought friends she didn't know, my sister would hide certain things that decorated the house in the closet. I never understood who would want the crap she was hiding, until now. Nothing is sacred, not even the crap!

Now that I've had money stolen from one of my tables to pay for a bottle of water that the people ordered, but couldn't afford anyway, then received a tip of an old, yet relative, hangman napkin – I figured, logic is out the door. It couldn't possibly get much worse. Never even think to yourself that things couldn't get worse! This should be rule number three in your life, right after never hit a woman and always use a condom. That should be the moral of the story, because Murphy's Law applies three times as strong in the hospitality industry than anywhere else in the world!

ISN'T THERE A BETTER WAY TO IDOLIZE SOMEONE?

It was Nascar week. We had the normal crowds, at the normal times, with the normal class levels. When I say class, I mean they have the kind of class undisputed by the normal man. Nothing points this out better when someone sits down at a dirty table to smoke a cigarette, and before you can get to them, uses a martini glass as an ashtray. If you, Joe-Bob have ever done this, stop it! Use the floor! We'll sweep it up! I know it isn't as fun, but come on, people have to drink out of those glasses! I'll get more into that in a couple pages; I just wanted to classify just whom I deal with.

After one of our rushes, we had a break, which was great because I had to go potty really bad. I grabbed the comics (#2) and head for, well, the head. Tired and frustrated, I did my business. When I reached up to dispense some ass wipe, I noticed a sticker

WHAT THE HELL IS WRONG WITH YOU!?

that seemed pretty new to it's location. It was on the side of the ass wipe dispenser. You know those 3" x 4" labels that you can buy at your local grocery store. They're usually printed with the phrase 'Hi, My name is'? Those are the ones that I'm talking about. Someone actually took stickers like these, that didn't have that title on them, and made his or her own. These stickers had a very generic border on the edges, showing that you could probably find these labels anywhere. On these stickers, someone had written a decorative symbol know by only some. I've never been a big pro wrestling fan, but one of my roommates is. This is the only way I would have known what 'Y2J' was. It's the nickname of a pro wrestler. Don't get me wrong; we all have our heroes. Of course, not all of them are in the sports entertainment industry. The thing that confuses me is this: What would possess someone to make homemade stickers, praising a pro wrestler, and stick them...in the shithouse...at the airport? Granted, it is a high traffic area, but what are you really saying about your hero? It wasn't like there was just one, either. There was a whole bunch stuck in different stalls in strategic places for better viewing.

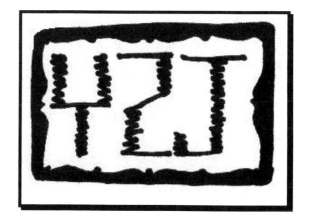

What The Hell Is Wrong With You!?

I guess I don't really understand. Sure, I'm a huge Phoenix Coyotes fan; so I wear a Coyotes jersey. I'm a big Alice In Chains fan; so I have an Alice In Chains sticker on the back window of my car. I've never, ever thought to advertise my pride of being a fan in the bathroom at the airport.

After about a week or two goes by, the stickers remained untouched. Evidentially, one day, probably someone who isn't much of a 'Y2J' fan, ripped down the stickers. Seeing that they were up there for a couple of weeks, they were stuck on there pretty good. You could tell because only half of the sticker actually came off. How do I know it wasn't a janitor, prêt ell? Easy. The other ones that remained, probably because they were so stuck on their surfaces the perpetrator couldn't get a corner up, were scribbled out with a black marker. This is when you should realize that maybe it has become a disorder. If you are wondering which of the two rivaling fans I am talking about, feel free to draw your own conclusions.

Why I Don't Live In Kentucky

This story touches my heart so much. It glows with love and human compassion.

This guy walks up to the bar. He's dressed in a red, long sleeved flannel shirt and overalls. His hair is longer and really messy like he just got off of the airplane...wing. I ask him what he would like to drink and in a slow southern drawl, he returns, "I want a strawberry margarita."

"Would you like a double shot for two dollars?" I asked in confusion. You see, I didn't expect this guy to order anything remotely frou-frou. I actually figured he would ask me for some jet fuel with a paper umbrella so he can watch it dissolve in his drink.

WHAT THE HELL IS WRONG WITH YOU!?

He agreed to the extra shot, so I went to the blender to make his drink. When he got his drink, he drank it slowly using the straw. Completely unexpected! A few minutes later, I returned to him and asked how he was doing. He complained that he couldn't taste any alcohol and asked me if I had put any in at all. I was sure that I put in two shots of alcohol, but normally when you order a drink like that, and the drink doesn't have the overwhelming taste of alcohol, that means I did my job right. It's just like the hundred thousand or so people that I've made a long island iced tea for that has said, "Did you put any alcohol in this? It tastes just like iced tea!"

I can't explain why it tastes like iced tea. It contains mostly alcohol, sour mix, and Coke. If the drink ever goes through a name change, maybe 'iced tea' should be in the name somewhere. What do you think about that? I'm getting off track, back to the story.

I finally negotiated him down to saying that I only put in one shot, even though I put in two. I told him the next drink he orders, not only will I pour it in front of him, but I will put his extra shot on the side. He agrees. When he orders his next drink, he says the 'extra shot idea' isn't going to work because he wants a piña colada instead. Perplexed again, I told him that I still could put the extra shot on the side; it would just be rum instead of tequila. I don't think he understood, but said okay anyhow. I made his piña colada and put his extra shot in a small highball glass. Quite honestly, it was a pretty big shot, too.

"Side shot? You call that a shot? No wonder I didn't taste any alcohol in the first one!" He complained. Now that I'm upset, I tried to hold my composure and told him to hang on a second. I walked down to the end of the bar and grabbed your typical shot glass and slammed it down in front of him.

"I'll tell you what," I said calmly, still smiling, "I'll take that shot back and pour it in this shot glass, which will only hold one legal shot of liquid. Whatever overflows from the shot glass and spills all over the bar, you can't have anymore. Would that be better for you?"

He picks up the empty shot glass, inspects it and asks, "Are you sure this is a shot glass?"

"Yes, I'm sure."

"I can't believe how small everything is here, especially for the prices you charge. I'll tell you what, you'd better never go to Kentucky."

"It wasn't in my life-long plans, but why's that?" I asked in curiosity.

"If you were a bartender in Kentucky, **we'd shoot you**." He said to me sternly as he scowled at me through his strait, Chris Gaines like hair that was now covering his face.

Okay, I know that Arizona liquor laws are a little strict, but holy shit! Isn't <u>shooting</u> a bartender illegal in all of the states!? Regardless, I'll heed the warning and stay right the hell away from Kentucky. I'll go to Oklahoma. I've heard it's *OK*.

HAVE YOU HEARD OF A LIQUOR STORE?

This quality is also found in many of the Joe-Bobs I've waited on before. I remember once at a bar that I used to work at, I exclaimed to my friend Joe, "Give me a Jack and Coke and put some stank on it!" When I said it, I said it to a friend of mine and I didn't really mean it – it was a joke. He did make it quite *stanky*, but he would have anyhow. This is as guilty of this I have ever been. The crime being when Joe-Bob orders mixed drinks and asks for more than one shot of alcohol in the drink. Normal people would call that a double. However, Joe-Bob makes it apparent that he wants a double, just doesn't want to pay for it.

WHAT THE HELL IS WRONG WITH YOU!?

My friend Joe Meranda, who is a bartender at McDuffy's in Tempe has a good answer for this situation. I was there for one of those situations:

"Make sure you put a lot of alcohol in my drink!" One belligerent, yet sober patron exclaimed.

"That must mean that you're going to give me a really big tip!" Joe replied laughing. This was the first and only time I saw a response to this that immediately shut the person up.

Me, on the other hand, have always had a problem even mentioning the word tip to some of these people just because of the fact that it would probably rile me up into an argument about how uncouth they actually are.

* * *

This one happened to me at a bar in a Mexican restaurant that I used to work at just a little while ago. Two guys (having the physical characteristics of a Joe-Bob) sat down at the bar. One ordered a beer and the other ordered a Jack and Coke. Right after the one on the left ordered the Jack and Coke, he said my three favorite words, and 'hook it up!' Most people know what 'hook it up' usually leads to; for those of you who don't, hang tight, it's explained in detail in chapter eleven.

As I walked over to the well, he yelled, loudly, "Hey man, Can you put in more whiskey?"

This is just stupid. The bar that we were in was a quieter, smaller bar. I was thinking of many things at that point. Who is this guy? He wants me to steal for him. He's not a pretty girl. He's not even a girl. Why the hell is he in a bar? Should I have him make his own drink? No, that would be bad.

Now that he has alerted any manager within earshot of his desire for me to not only break policies, but to break liquor laws, he continues. After seeing me pour a four-second shot from the bottle, he yelled, "Could you hook up my drink more, man?"

What The Hell Is Wrong With You!?

This wasn't enough. I brought his drink over and he said, "I saw you pour it, could you give me a good shot?"

"That was a good shot." I exclaimed, now miffed and not wanting to give him any more alcohol.

"Well, could you add more?"

"Would you like a double?"

"No, just remember it for next time."

I just turned around to the computer going into 'ignorance is bliss' mode. I then heard him say, "You know, this one is okay." Uh-huh.

The time came (quickly) for him to order his second Jack and Coke.

"I'm sorry, man, I didn't mean to make you nervous before. Can I get another drink and could you turn it up?"

Nervous? *Turn it up*? First of all, it wasn't a nervous situation, just nerve racking. And 'turn it up'? Listen to Lynard Skynard do you? Is that *Freedom Rock*, man? Yeah, man! Well turn it up man! (Sorry.)

Just so he would shut up, I pretended to put in a larger shot by holding my thumb over the pour spout and holding the bottle upside down. This drink had the same amount of alcohol as the first one.

"Yeah, that's what I'm talkin' about!" The guy said after he sipped to assess the value of his second drink. He didn't even notice that it was the same as the first. At least he thought I 'hooked it up'. I doubted that it would have helped my tip any, that is if I was to receive one at all.

I actually wondered if this certain procedure could work in other situations or other businesses. I think I'll try it once. I'll go to the bank to make a deposit and say, "Hey, could you throw in an extra $20 into my account? Could you *hook it up* for me? Come on, it's not your money anyway!"

WHAT THE HELL IS WRONG WITH YOU!?

When they received their bill, they only had a total of four drinks. Their bill was about $20. This wasn't bad for happy hour prices on the beer, two Jack and Cokes, an appetizer from the kitchen and free chips and salsa. Not only did they leave me a total of $22 dollars, but left a chip, water, and salsa catastrophe two feet in each direction of their previous location. Yippee! Ten-percent tip AND I get to clean up a huge mess! That makes up for all the pestering from before! It's like – I scratch your back, you break a 2×4 across mine. Thanks, that's great.

* * *

I have a message for all the people that are like this. Many bars don't free-pour (measure alcohol by counting); they use stopper-pours or jiggers. If you want really strong drinks, but don't want to pay the high prices, go to a liquor store. You can buy a whole bottle of anything you want and mix it up yourself – as strong as you want it! Hell, you could drink it right out of the bottle; I don't care!

FOUR RULES FOR JOE-BOB TO FOLLOW

I guess, all through life, I will always run into these types of people, and so will you. One of the worst things that I've ever had to keep a strait face through was when a man in his late thirties, wearing nicer farm-like clothing, pointed to the margarita menu and said, "In yer educated opinion, which one of these here margaritas is gooder?"

Actually, I can't lie, I laughed my ass off at him; I couldn't help it. Just in case, I looked up the word in my handy little spell checker. It said that I should be trying to say guider, gadder (one whom roams about - gadabout), gaudier, gooier, Goddess, or Judy. Not once did it say 'better'.

The good thing about this, even though it would most certainly be difficult, you can help some of these people.

WHAT THE HELL IS WRONG WITH YOU!?

Unfortunately, we will never help them all, and that's a shame. I'd like you to notice as well that I can't break this genre of our species down to one specific region of the country. It's a proven fact; they are everywhere. Sure, there are larger segments of these people per capita in certain areas, but I won't point out any states in particular – *OK*? If you ever worry whether or not you are in this category, let me sum it up for you to make you a better person:

1. When you are finished with your chewing gum, do not, ever dispose of it under a chair or table thinking that no one will ever find it. It's due to assholes like you that servers and bartenders all over the world have the shit-job of scrapping your gum off of the damnedest places. If we are lucky enough not to have this shit-job on a list somewhere, it's still found when we go to move a table and our index finger squishes into a nice fresh piece of supersaturated chewing medium. Keep in mind that on packages of gum, it states 'keep gum wrapper for disposal of used gum'. This simply means to keep the wrapper, which came with the gum, to dispose of the gum when you're done, as in, to throw away! If you had lost the wrapper, don't fret; you can use a napkin. <u>You can find napkins at every bar and restaurant</u>. Also, while on the subject of gum, please do not throw gum away in your drink glass. Not only is this incredibly unsanitary (that means un-healthy-like), the gum comes off in the brushes used to clean the glassware behind the bar. The gum usually circulates through all five spinning brushes like how the cotton candy goes on the stick at the fair. I know you know what I'm talking about. Not only does this transpire into a nightmare of hellish cleaning resembling the time my lasagna exploded in the microwave, but slows down the whole bar process for about a half an hour. I shouldn't have to tell anyone not to just throw gum on the floor. I think we all know that one. At times when I step in gum, it makes

me feel better to think that maybe it just fell off the bottom off a table.

2. Like I mentioned before, do not use a glass as an ashtray. If you need to smoke that bad, there are alternatives. Find an ashtray. I know, what a novel idea when you're in a smoking bar. Or go outside. Now before anyone jumps down my throat about littering and the environment, I will go in depth on this idea. When you are done, throw your cigarette butts in the garbage (important: make sure it's not still lit!). A little side note here: Not to confuse any of my friends on the east coast that call unused cigarettes 'butts', you can smoke it before you throw it out. Or you can do the safest thing and abstain; it's healthier for you!

3. Never, I repeat, **never** stand up at the bar and eat out of the fruit tray. This too is unsanitary. I know that maraschino cherries and Spanish olives with the pimentos are not just tasty, exotic, and right at hand, but they are for the drinks. The fruit tray is not a complimentary salad bar! If you want something out of there, just ask. I'd say, on a good day, 80 percent of the time, the bartender will give you a rocks glass of olives, or cherries, or whatever. If you do this, you will also notice that he or she will not deplete the available supply because, yes, once again, he or she will need them **for the drinks**. I mean, if you were to find this acceptable, why wouldn't you just go back to the kitchen and eat celery that comes with wings? Or better yet, sit back there and eat all the parsley or kale used for decoration on the plates! Or even better yet...**don't!** Just in case you wonder why this bothers me so much, listen to this: Numerous times I have had people in this class, usually by them selves, stand next to the fruit tray and eat damn near everything in it. Of course, if I notice, I'll tell them how gross they are and do the rocks glass thing. If I don't notice, if they are sneaky enough, eventually I will notice when someone orders a martini and I don't have any fucking olives left. Then I get the pleasure of looking over to the person still chewing with a bright red pimento sticking out of his or her fat mouth as they smile like they didn't do anything wrong. Now I have to go get more from the cooler in back, further wasting my time. So then, if you're hungry, order food. If there is no food served wherever you are hungry, hit a fast food joint on the way home. Thank you.

4. Last, but not least, please, for the love of all that is holy, do not ask for things for free. It's so damn tacky; you could hang posters (get it?). If you are lucky enough to get something for free out of promotion, or a friend takes care of you, that's great! Enjoy it! I have not yet met a restaurant employee that enjoys hearing non-leveraged negotiations for a free beer *or something*. Every bar that I've been to before have had specials of some kind, even at the airport. Be happy that you have that instead of trying to barter for a quantity discount.

So, for future reference, if you are one of the special ones, follow the four things that I've listed above. From here on out, you'll be golden. See people, I'm just trying to help.

What The Hell Is Wrong With You!?

Chapter Numero Diez:
Pricing Structures ~ It's Not My Fault!

I'm going to start off this entire chapter with advice for all. This is something that I have wanted to say to half the people that come into the airport bar. For future reference, if you ever find yourself at any kind of sporting event, Las Vegas, music concert, rodeo, hotel, motel, resort, art festival, renaissance festival, anything else ending in the word 'festival', fairs or amusement parks, or (especially) an airport; expect to spend a lot of money on anything consumable. You can usually get away with finding cheap inedible objects, but I wouldn't advise eating or drinking items like key chains or little figurines of animals.

I run into people everyday that are just amazed that a drink could cost six to eight dollars. I've even had a woman get upset and yell at me because her glass of (crap) chardonnay cost her $5.69. She told me that wine doesn't even cost that much where she lives, in California. Oh yeah, that's right, I forgot, everything is <u>cheaper</u> on the west coast. She actually wound up complaining to the manager about the prices and how ridiculous they are. That's right, she got everything for free. The best part is I didn't get a tip because it's obviously my fault that stuff is expensive at the airport! Once again rides the glorified busboy.

While I'm on the subject, I would like to bring up something that everyone should take advantage of. If you have ever been drinking in a bar in almost any airport, you have probably heard the 'special deal' that has lasted for over ten years. If not, then you will hear it now. If you order a beer, you can get a shot of liquor for two dollars. If you get a mixed drink, you can get a double shot in the drink for two dollars. Take it! This is the most economical thing for you to do. Figure that you are going to spend some money anyway – because you will regardless. But if

WHAT THE HELL IS WRONG WITH YOU!?

you do get the extra shot (or shots), your tab will look like any tab from any typical bar instead of a tab where you could expect a complimentary side of Vaseline™.

* * *

Now don't do what some people do and misconstrue what I said above about a 'double for two dollars'. This doesn't mean that you get the whole drink for two dollars. This happens a lot. I'll bring someone his or her double Jack and Coke, and they'll toss me three dollars. I understand that I did say 'double for two dollars', but if you really thought the double was two dollars, would you think a single shot drink is only a buck? At the airport! Hell, you can't even get one of those rental luggage carts at the airport for a dollar let alone a drink at a bar!? I can't believe how people can mentally accept this without being skeptical. I've actually had conversations like this:

"How much do you get for a Jack and Coke?"

"$6.76," I replied, "you can get a double shot for two dollars."

"So the price goes down if I get a double?" They said shaking their head like an excited puppy dog.

"No."

Does that make any sense to anyone? Is there a place on earth that you could order a drink only to find the more alcohol that goes into the drink, the lesser the price? Don't get me wrong, it sounds wonderful in theory, even deadly in practice, but probably not very good for a business owner; nor a server or bartender working on a percentage. If you don't know what I mean by percentage, proceed to the next chapter on tipping.

What The Hell Is Wrong With You!?

Your Money Goes In The Cash Drawer, Not My Pocket ~ You Moron!

If you ever go someplace and find that everything is unconditionally expensive, don't bitch about the price and then stiff the server or bartender. I can guarantee that they had absolutely nothing to do with it. If you are in a place that can afford to have its prices that high, the owners are not working. They might be there, but they'd be drinking and laughing. I've had people here and there say stupid fucked up things to *me* like, "I'd leave you a better tip if your prices weren't so damn high."

I even doubt the sincerity behind that statement because if you told that person to wait and then give them, say, the cost of one beer back; I'd bet you that he would just take it, shove it in his pocket, and walk away. He wouldn't even say thanks. Some people are just shitty like that.

There have also been times that, after I tell them how much their tab is, they say something like, "Yeah, you sure are making a killing on me, aren't you?"

You know you're getting a good tip then! I say that because, by the statements they make and the tips they have left before, they actually think that a buddy and I got together one day and opened a bar AT THE AIRPORT! Think, please!

What Prices Really Include

I will be the first to tell you that there are many situations and geographical regions that will just rip you off when in comes to prices. However, I do need to stick up for the normal restaurants out there. I actually try to remind customers of these basic facts that are taken for granted when they bitch about a cup of coffee costing two dollars. Some of these things are kind of

WHAT THE HELL IS WRONG WITH YOU!?

cheesy to be brought up, but all of the following things cost money. If you think that all of the two dollars for that coffee goes right to the restaurateur's pocket, you are not too smart. I'm actually sharing this with you so you can use it in your defense to feel better when you know from their bitching, you're not getting a tip.

o Ambiance
o Use of furniture, cups, glasses, plates and flatware
o Replacement of furniture, cups, glasses, plates and flatware
o Cleaning of furniture, cups, glasses, plates and flatware
o All the napkins you use
o The ass-wipe in the bathroom
o Soap and other cleaning aids
o Aesthetic value – decoration for your poor, abused eyes
o Refrigeration so you don't eat rotten food
o The cost of the product your consuming
o Air conditioning or heating – that's never free
o Service – even though we're paid poorly, we are paid
o Labor for the cooks, dishwashers, managers, security, etc
o Less aggravation because <u>we</u> clean up your disaster areas
o Smoke eaters (when applicable) give you clean air
o Anything audio/visual – music, television, satellite, etc
o Water
o Condiments
o Fruits and vegetables used as garnish

I'm sure there's more, but these are the ones that I could think of right away. If you need to fill in more, feel free. If this list doesn't help you, then tell the unruly customers to stop at a convenience store, buy a six-pack, and go right the hell home.

WHAT THE HELL IS WRONG WITH YOU!?

IF YOU ARE A FRUGAL PERSON, MAYBE THE AIRPORT ISN'T A GOOD PLACE TO DRINK

There have been people that try to be cute with the whole 'two-dollar' thing. I would ask them if they would like a shot for two dollars with their beer. They would then say something like, "Oh, you're just trying to get me drunk, aren't you?"

Now, if a cute girl says this to me, then the answer is 'yes, of course'. But if not, my answer is always, "No, I'm going to rip you off on the price of the beer, you might as well get some value added while you have the opportunity."

It's amazing how people will try to save such little amounts of money when they are drinking at the airport. The sentence I just wrote here <u>does</u> make sense, until you break it down. This will explain my incredulity. If you really wanted to save money, why the hell would you drink at the airport!? What I mean is that if you're not on vacation or a business trip where you know you were going to spend money, why drink at the airport? And if you do decide to drink at the airport, even on a budget, splurge. Treat yourself. You're going to be spending a pretty penny anyhow, you know? If it is a necessity for some, then they should invest in a flask and save money that way. I guess maybe that's just what I would do.

An example of this shows that someone is willing to pay a great deal for a drink at the bar, but not to go that extra mile. Someone ordered an Absolute and tonic once.

"Would you like a double for two dollars?" I asked.

They actually understood what I meant and asked, "How much would that make it?"

"$8.91," I answered. You wouldn't believe how quick some people that ASKED for the expensive stuff would go strait from frill to swill.

What The Hell Is Wrong With You!?

"I'll just have your well vodka then."

Little did they know that our well vodka is Smirnoff and will still cost them $7.84. Oh well.

Last Of The Big Spenders?

This is a word of advice for all those people that like to talk big only to later find themselves using their credit card to pry their foot from their mouth. If you go into a restaurant or bar anywhere in the world that has a Mexican theme, never order this, "A round of shots, for me and all of my amigos, your finest tequila!"

I will guarantee you the Mexican restaurants' finest tequila will not cost around five dollars a shot. It might not even be less that ten. As a matter of fact, I have been to a few <u>normal</u> Mexican restaurants before, hanging out at the bar looking at their tequila menus. I found that if I were to say that same sentence with only two of my friends with me, the shots alone would be just over three hundred dollars. It's not an odd thing to find hundred dollar shots of tequila, even outside of Arizona, Texas, and California. True, you may not be able to find expensive tequila where people don't even know what a taco is (take-oh!). But I guess we'll never know.

So you know, this applies with more than just tequilas. There are numerous types of wine, beer, and alcohols that will fit this classification. Always ask how much 'the most expensive' is. The main reason is this: There are some bartenders, servers, and managers that will not tell you how much the most expensive is and just serve it with a smile stretched from ear to ear. They will just assume you already know how much it is. At the prices I used as an example, they may even sing and dance for you! When you get angry because the bill is so high, they may stop singing and dancing, but they will still make you pay.

What The Hell Is Wrong With You!?

Pay Your Tab ~ Loser

This is something that happens everywhere on occasion, but at the airport, it's almost a daily occurrence. This is when people leave without paying. People that walk out on their tabs are the scummiest, crappiest, most worthless, cheap pieces of trash ever to waste the air that I breathe. I'm pretty emphatic about that. There are a few types of people that do this.

One type will plan to go to a bar, get pickled, and leave when no one's looking. These people are the worst!

Then there are the types of idiots, more so, but not exclusive to the airport, who just leave because they can't wait up to a minute for a check. They figure that even though they are in a busy restaurant, if they don't have their check sitting in front of them, then it must be free. Hey, guess what, you suck! I've had people ask me for their check because they were in a big hurry, and as I printed it, they would leave. I don't feel I have to remind you that you were in a sit-down restaurant. I do have a solution to fix this little bad habit. Estimate how much your bill would be and leave some money behind. Even if you're short, it's so much better than just leaving, dirt bag.

The other types are the people that get so stewed that they just forget to pay. Even though I have never done that before (to my recollection, that is, maybe I have) I can kind of understand. This type isn't necessarily 'trash'. My apologies.

Now, let me tell you why these people are such stinky pieces of shit – flies wouldn't approach. Half of the bars that I've worked in do not have any sort of 'walkout' clause. They say you should always get a credit card to hold an open tab. Good advice, if you're not busy, or when nobody would be able to sneak out. To top it off, I can't hold on to a bunch of credit cards because I would lose them. What I would have to do is take the credit card and start

What The Hell Is Wrong With You!?

a tab in the credit card machine. It's either that, take your chances, or go 'cash-and-carry' on everything, even food. Also, if you ask one table for a credit card, you need to ask everyone for a credit card so that no one feels discriminated against. Welcome to the crazy sue-happy 21st century! I have spent, throughout the years, I'd say up to $500 in unpaid bar tabs because people would just leave. Okay, I admit it is partially my fault for not grabbing a credit card from every table, but on these upcoming, example occasions, it was so busy that I just couldn't. I know it's not just me either. Everyone that I used to work with at these certain jobs would have walkouts and have to pay for them as well. Sometimes we would all get a pool together to lessen the burden on the server or bartender. This also shows the good family like structure that restaurant employees can bond by. Some of these losers don't understand that most restaurant employees live on their tips – even me. I've had nights before where I would have made a hundred dollars working all night long until two in the morning. But, because two people were shit-fucks, I had to pay for their $77 tab. After that, I got to go home with $23 fucking dollars to add to my 'rent fund'. Let me tell you another story because it still pisses me off how everything went down.

Monday Night Shit-Fucks

These two schmucks came in and sat down at about four o'clock on a Monday night. We were not busy at the time. I could have, but did not get a credit card. I had two reasons not to. One, people that come in at the beginning of happy hour usually won't last until kickoff of the Monday Night Football game. And two, they looked like they had money and were not concerned about losing it. They had cell phones on the table and were dressed well, etc. Little did I know how much concern they lacked. My mistake.   They were also betting on the dog races with the available off track betting. They had pitcher after pitcher of beer and shots every half an hour. They also reassured me that someone was going to come pick them up during half time of the game to drive them home. They got drunk. Not to the point that I would have to cut them off, but close. When half time began, a woman came in a joined them at the table. She was given a beer glass, but didn't drink much at all. I would say about a half a glass of beer. I went back to grab some food from the kitchen. When I returned, the schmucks were gone, the girl was gone, and the cell phones were gone.

"Son of a bitch!" I exclaimed to myself as I ran out the front door to catch them. I ran straight out through the patio and into the parking lot. As soon as my eyeball's field of vision got to the left side of my head as I scanned the parking lot, I saw them. They were in a black two-door Jaguar with tinted windows. The car started accelerating towards me before the last person could get all the way into the car. The door slammed shut due to the forward movement. As they blew by me, I jumped back to avoid being hit by the car. As they zoomed by, I looked into the car and saw the woman with ramen-like hair and two guys all crammed in the cabin like they just jumped into the clown car at the circus right before being announced. Incidentally, the woman that seemed sober and wasn't drinking at my bar was driving. So, they did have a designated driver, or getaway car – what have you.

They didn't even look out onto the road when they bolted into the far lane, across two other lanes. Luckily for others, no one was coming down the road. I watched them speed out of sight with their left rear light burnt out.

As they sped away, I got the license plate number. I'm enraged at this point, but feeling helpless, I go back inside. When I went back inside, I found that the rest of my tables were all looking for me because they all needed something. So, thanks to Murphy, while the rat bastards are getting away, I'm now completely slammed.

About an hour later, I finally get the chance to call the police. About an hour after that, they arrive to take my report. I tell them everything and gave descriptions on everybody involved and the car. I was told, seeing that it's been over two hours, it would be pointless to send out an all points bulletin (APB, for you chronic *Cops* watchers) and all they could do with the license plate number is this. Now, read this slow because it's great:

- First they would have to call in the license plate number to see if it's registered in Arizona and if it's current. (Okay...)
- Then, they would have to cross check the license plate number with the department of motor vehicles to see if the license plate matches closely to my description of the vehicle. (Okay, let's do it...)
- Finally, they would write a letter from the court informing the person, whose name appears on the registration, of what had happened. (Good idea, get the bad guy!)
- And last, **the person whose name appears on the registration for the car would have to <u>ADMIT BLAME</u> to the crime depicted in the letter.** (What the shit!?)

I've never been much of a thief. I think it's due to a traumatic childhood experience when I was busted by a grocery store rent-a-cop with two pockets full of Starburst. I actually don't like thieves at all. Especially the ones that have taken shit from me. However, if I was a thief, and I got away with the crime and then, say, two months later I received a letter asking me if I did it, yes or no; I wonder if I would turn myself in, or maybe just laugh myself to death. This is why I loathe these people so very much. I don't like to hate, you know? So if you know these people, could

What The Hell Is Wrong With You!?

you punch them in the face for me? I know it's probably a little too much to ask, but it would make me feel better. Thank you!

Now that I'm upset, I'll try to calm down by telling you a few funnier things that I have heard in the industry about prices.

Cheesy Joke For You

Something that I do when someone complains about how expensive the tab is this: Take the ticket back and tell them that you're going to take a little off the top. I know it's cheesy, but it takes the edge off so you don't have to hear a bunch of people complaining about the prices. Take the ticket and rip off the top part of the check right above the name of the bar, fold in nicely and hand it back to them. When you hand it back, walk away so they don't look at you like you're an idiot. It's usually good for a couple laughs. Either way.

Someone Else Who's On The Verge Of Cracking Under The Pressure

This is a quick little story that I had to add in at the last minute because it was so damn funny when I heard it. Of course, I was drunk at the time, but I think it's still funny now.

One of my friends, Margie Sierra, works at a nightclub called the Bash on Ash in Tempe. There are some nights with certain events that either don't bring in many people, or bring in droves of bad tippers. This story exemplifies how close restaurant employees are to come back to some of your annoyances.

Someone walked up to Margie and tried to order a drink. It was instantly apparent that he didn't have much money to spend and therefore, shouldn't go out

What The Hell Is Wrong With You!?

"How much are your domestic beers?" The customer asked. Margie answered like she would to anyone.

"How much are your mixed drinks?" He said. Margie answered with some wonder about where he was going with this. Then the customer voiced his true intentions:

"What's the cheapest thing you have in the bar?"

"It's you mother fucker!" Margie said back.

Reasonable Comebacks

The other things I have here are a few quotes that others have said about the prices that I couldn't help but to add them in:

Once when I was serving at the airport, I had a table of about twenty guys on their way to Mexico. They were all business like people dressed in casual attire. You know, un-faded jeans, tacky Hawaiian pattern shirts, and penny loafers. The usual. They all seemed to be really cool.

They seemed to all agree, some more reluctantly than others, to start their Mexican vacation early. On their first round of drinks, they were using the two-dollar shot and double thing to their advantage. They had about an hour to wait so they ordered a few baskets of chips and salsa with their second round of drinks. On their third round, they seemed to calm down some. They were drinking a little slower and didn't seem to keen on chasing down any more shots. The apparent leader of the group asked me to see if anyone else needed another beer before he closed the tab. He told me to bring the entire tab to him.

After the group consumed numerous shots of tequila followed closely by an entourage of Mexican beers and margaritas, the leader then *unfolded* the tab. He only had a few margaritas before he saw the check, but his sticker-shock reaction was priceless. He looked at the silenced table as he held the two-foot long tab in both hands. He exclaimed, "$265!? Holy shit! It would have been cheaper just to buy Mexico!"

* * *

I was washing glassware when I overheard one of the other bartenders' conversations with a customer at the bar. The customer was one of those older guys that you would find spending most of his time in a little hole in the wall bar. He looked like the type of guy that would always have a good story to tell or something funny to say. Unfortunately for me, he was more interested in the ball game on TV to small talk with anyone.

He ordered his beer and nursed it while he watched the game. Halfway through his second beer, he asked the other bartender how much each beer cost. The bartender answered $5.15. I didn't hear him very well, but I know that he primarily gave one of the aforementioned natural impulse answers like, "I could buy a whole six pack for that," or, "Do I get to keep the glass, too?" (Again, what the hell is it with the glassware!?) Regardless, I wasn't serving him so it was of very little importance to me. He then came around with one that made me pay more attention, to laugh. The other bartender came back to him a little later and asked if he wanted another beer. He slowly lost his interlocked gaze with the big screen and told the other bartender, "Yeah, you know, I might as well have another beer," then he started to mumble to himself, "Before the prices get raised any higher!"

* * *

The moral of the stories that I've told above is as follows. I've heard this from at least twelve coworkers from each job that I've ever had before that involves tips. If you know it's going to be really expensive, plan to spend some money. This includes the proper gratuity. If you don't have the money to go drinking and leave a tip, don't go drinking. Words of wisdom that bring me right into the next chapter.

What The Hell Is Wrong With You!?

Chapter Numero Once (Chapter 11, Go Figure)
Tipping ~ The Etiquette Behind The Legend

Handy-Dandy Tip Chart

Check Total	15%	17%	20%
$8.50	$1.28	$1.45	$1.70
$10.50	$1.58	$1.79	$2.10
$12.50	$1.88	$2.13	$2.50
$15.50	$2.33	$2.64	$3.10
$17.50	$2.63	$2.98	$3.50
$20.00	$3.00	$3.40	$4.00
$25.00	$3.75	$4.25	$5.00
$30.00	$4.50	$5.10	$6.00
$35.00	$5.25	$5.95	$7.00
$40.00	$6.00	$6.80	$8.00
$45.00	$6.75	$7.65	$9.00
$50.00	$7.50	$8.50	$10.00
$60.00	$9.00	$10.20	$12.00
$75.00	$11.25	$12.75	$15.00
$90.00	$13.50	$15.30	$18.00
$100.00	$15.00	$17.00	$20.00
$120.00	$18.00	$20.40	$24.00
$150.00	$22.50	$25.50	$30.00
$200.00	$30.00	$34.00	$40.00
$43,720.00	$6,558.00	$7,432.40	$8,744.00

There are so many ways to start this chapter; I don't even know where to begin. I guess I will start with the most important aspect of tipped employees. That's exactly what we are – tipped

WHAT THE HELL IS WRONG WITH YOU!?

employees. I want everyone in the world to know this because I don't think that many people do. Here's a good example:

I was 19 years old when I told my own mother that she should tip when she goes out to restaurants. I had recently moved back home to Phoenix and went to lunch with my mom. At the time, I was a server at Jaybeez restaurants. Right before that, I was at Heckel's restaurants in Chippewa Falls, Wisconsin. Both of these jobs, I had made $2.13 to $2.33 per hour, plus tips. My own mother, none the wiser to that fact, had been tipping nothing to a couple of bucks, depending on whether the service was spectacular or not. I told her, like I've mentioned a couple times already; 80 to 90 percent of a restaurant workers wages are from their tips. Not tipping them is like going to a normal nine-to-five job and working for free one day out of the week. Okay, that's a bit outlandish, but that's how we all feel when we give good service and receive nothing in return.

I do know that there are some areas of the country that hold restaurant workers in a union. These people also fit into this category of those whom still deserve to be tipped. There are two reasons for this. Number one; They still live on their tips because their hourly wages pay for their taxes, union dues, and other things that you need to do and buy just to work in a union. Number two; normally, they have had to work in the industry for YEARS, in that same union, on a part time basis to get to the position that they are at.

I honestly believe that you should tip everyone that gives you a service of any kind. This should include (but not limited to) haircuts, auto work (unless they're hosing you on labor costs), the car wash guys, strippers, bellboys, flight attendants, anyone that drives you anywhere in a vehicle with wheels, doormen, and especially, restaurant workers. For all of you service industry people that I've left out, I'm sorry; you can scribble your occupation in the margin. I'll vouch for you!

What The Hell Is Wrong With You!?

Just in case you didn't know, this industry has a big foundation on tipping. If no one tipped, no one would be around to serve you on a day-to-day basis. Nobody's that happy, unless they're drugged. If you go into a bar or restaurant, expect to have to tip, or pay the consequences. These consequences could vary from being ignored to someone accidentally pouring an entire pitcher of sticky soda on you. I have yet to do this, but the thought has still crossed my mind numerous times. I wouldn't even get stuck with the dry cleaning bill. Vindictive? Yes. Practical? No, not really. Would it make me feel better? Oh, hell yes! Keep these things in mind if you are, in fact, an idiot.

For myself, if I'm in a restaurant, I will tip well. I also tip accordingly. If the service is really bad, then, because I've worked in the business for so long, I'll only tip 15%, but I will never stiff. Personally, I would rather have a nice kick in the pants than a proverbial slap in the face by someone stiffing me.

If, on the other hand, the service is good, or especially if they did something entertaining or extraordinary to make my experience that much better, they will probably get an outstanding tip; no matter where I am.

I don't make all that much money, but I do stick to what I say about tipping everyone that gives a service. I remember this one time, not to long ago; I went to a Jiffy Lube. I was too damn lazy and hungover on my day off to change the oil in my car. I figured I would pay the extra ten bucks and have someone else do it. I pulled into the little drive through garage and the moment I stepped out of my car, they went to work like a professional pit crew. Of course, they didn't crash my car so they lost a couple of entertainment points right there (that was so uncalled for, I'm sorry). It was so interesting to watch all of them rotate around my car checking every fluid and pressure level and simultaneously filling them, if needed, right after being checked. The best part of

What The Hell Is Wrong With You!?

the show was when they buttoned everything back up and did a safety check before starting the car. Hearing them all sound off 'clear!' one by one like they were a swat team clearing a house in an action movie. I know that this is probably normal practice when working at one of these places, but seeing that I have one of the lowest entertainment values known to man, I was enthralled! I tipped them twenty dollars to go grab a round of beer when they were done because it was one of the most fascinating things that I've ever seen. Sad, I know. Shut up.

* * *

Now, this obviously does not hold true for everyone, but for the most part, it's a difficult thing discussing a tip with a customer. Whether it's someone asking you if a really good tip is enough, or if it's someone else whom you know isn't going to tip at all. It's an awkward thing. Therefore, I'll write a book.

Leftover Chump-Change Should Not Be Used As A Tip!

There are so many things that I've seen, heard about, and have done myself on occasion to the people that don't tip. I think Carla on the TV show *Cheers* said it best. Sam, the bartender, was scolding her for throwing change at a customer because it was her tip. Carla replied, "Yeah, but it was the correct change!" I've actually known quite a few people that have gone out into the parking lot to throw a tip of change back at the customers.

One of the bartenders at the airport told me a story about receiving change as a tip at a different bar that he used to work in. They would immediately pick up the change, look the customer that left it on the bar, and throw it forcefully behind them over their shoulders. They would maintain an uncomfortable stare as the coins would ricochet between the bottles of liquor on the shelf behind them.

WHAT THE HELL IS WRONG WITH YOU!?

I guess what I'm trying to spell out is that restaurant workers would rather be stiffed than given a tip of change. Even though it's a terrible thing to do to anyone, if you leave some change behind, it makes us think that you're cheap, if you stiff someone, than you're just ignorant (and maybe cheap too, but we'll think ignorant). Now then, I want to make it very clear that I'm not telling anyone to stiff tipped employees, use the tip chart!

I myself don't throw change back at people…yet, but I do make sure they get it. If someone goes up to the bar and orders a beer that costs $5.90, and they give me a five and a one, no matter how busy I am I will deliver the dime with the receipt to the person. I will do this even if I need to chase them to a table. Sometimes they will actually come back up to the bar and tip (further bettering mankind). Other times, people will come up to the bar, order their drinks and leave enough money for the drinks leaving just a little change leftover and RUN away from the bar before I or the other bartender can say anything. It's really bad when they show that they know they're doing something wrong.

Here is one of my favorite things to do when we are really busy and the bar becomes standing room only. One of the people that I just described will come up to the bar, leave a five-dollar bill for a beer that costs $4.83, and try to run away. This person usually won't be able to run away due to the wall-to-wall people standing around him. He will usually just stop abruptly, look around, then stare at a television avoiding eye contact with any of us like he never did anything wrong. However, sometimes they will keep digging themselves through the people to get away. This is when I will go to the register right away and bring back the 17 cents to where the person was and loudly announce, "Sir? You forgot your seventeen cents up here! Sir!"

Usually, the other people at the bar will turn around and look at the person as if to be thinking, "Tip them, jackass!" This look seems to have a good enough effect on the person. The same person will walk up and order himself another beer, *and then tip*. He will then look around for peer approval. Yeah, we knew he was just waiting for the second round to tip. Okay. Also, you will find that others at the bar that didn't tip you before are, all of a sudden, digging in their pockets to avoid 'the glares'.

Nickel's worth of free advice for you. If you tip the bartender or server well on the first round, even if you don't tip well on the second, you'll get better service. It's an old trick that will always work. Also, visa-versa, if you don't tip the first time, you will probably be put on the end of your server or bartender's priority list. It's nothing personal, it's just business.

* * *

Here's another scenario to substantiate that restaurant workers would rather be stiffed than tipped change. This is another true story that happens all of the time at the airport in particular. Someone will walk up to the bar and order a couple of drinks. There total will come to, let's say, $9.92. They will hand me a ten-dollar bill and carry the drinks away to a table. They will turn around and get my attention so that I can see them waive off the eight cents, as if to say, "No, go ahead, keep it, I don't need it." Again, I would rather be stiffed than be ridiculed with an eight-cent tip. Especially when the two bartenders pool the tips together. That means I only made four cents! That is so disrespectful to my industry that it makes me sick. I know that everyone else that I've ever worked with would agree. I'd bet that everyone else in the world would too.

What The Hell Is Wrong With You!?

We're Not Holding Your Food Hostage; You're Just In A 'Full Service Restaurant'.

Another atrocity is when people come into a really busy sit down restaurant and expect to be in and out within thirty minutes. This is expected a lot at the airport. This does not happen in a sit down restaurant. Even if you know exactly what you want, it's still a gamble. That thirty-minute idea was the pizza delivery thing, remember? What's more, when these people aren't in and out in thirty minutes, it's the server or bartender's fault. They will be penalized by not receiving a tip.

Before I get into examples of this, I would like to tell anyone out there who doesn't know this important piece of dining knowledge: I implore you, **If you don't have the time to sit down in a restaurant to eat, do not sit down in a restaurant to eat! This is why God gave us 'fast food establishments'!** I would once again like to point out the word 'fast' in the last sentence. This word is synonymous with 'it's already made and ready to eat'. If you ever find yourself in an airport, you will notice that there are more fast food establishments than sit down restaurants. I'm not sure why, I know that no one at the airport could possibly have a plane to catch. I think I would have heard about it by now.

Additionally, if you are ever in a bar in the airport and you see a frustrated redhead, with a red face to match, walking around quickly chanting, "Burger King, Burger King, that's what the Burger King is for!!" You will know that it's probably me.

What The Hell Is Wrong With You!?

Can't You Tell That We're Slammed And I'm Still Taking Care Of You?

Here's another thing that sends me right into anger management classes. This happens to me at the airport quite often. This one instance in particular happened only about a month ago. I was serving that day when we only had five servers working the tables. This is a perfect setup on a day that we knew was not going to be busy. Consequently, the weather in different destination cities had other plans in store for us. A couple flights were delayed for a little more than a half an hour. Out of nowhere, the entire bar filled up with people. I had, at one time; twelve tables sit down, pick up a menu, and have all of the people follow me around with their eyes like a bunch of pit bulls like I was carrying around a porterhouse! Usually, I will have no problem memorizing my orders, even with a steady flow of tables or customers. Writing slows me down. This was an unusually busy time. I grabbed a stack of napkins and started taking orders from one end of my station to the other. I would take three or four orders, go ring them in, then take three or four more, then run the first groups' drinks, and keep doing this in succession until everyone had what they ordered. I believe it's called 'consolidation verses cluster-fuck'.

In case you would not do this, or have not served before, know that if you ring in twelve tables food and drink orders all at the same time, you will be fucked. Drink number 3 will be dead by the time the bartender gets around to drink number 14. The kitchen, and I was a cook before too, so I know this for a fact, will take all twelve of your tickets and put them to the end.

Foremost and the best part is when you return to the first table with their drinks, you will notice that one of the people went up to the bar and ordered the same damn thing because it took too long (another pet peeve of mine, I'll touch up on it later). Not good for you. Not good for anyone.

WHAT THE HELL IS WRONG WITH YOU!?

Anyhow, I usually will not take food orders with the drink orders just because it's good practice to get everyone a drink, or something in front of them as soon as possible. Pacify the whinny little **adults** with something to suck on. Against my better judgment, I did take food orders with the drink orders because everyone only had thirty minutes. The all had (everyone together now!) a plane to catch.

As I was taking the third tier's orders, I noticed that one of my customers that I had just ordered walked up to the bar and waited in the server well for his family's drinks that I just rang in. Noble, but do not ever do this, ever!! Not only does it piss off your busy server that you might think you're doing a favor for, but if your server does not see you do it, they will have a time consuming fight with the bartender on where the server's drinks went. As a good rule of thumb: **stay out of the service well! You don't belong there!** You get in the way and cause chaos. The system exists for a reason; don't crash the system, please. I actually felt a little better when their food was ready. I walked up to the table without their food and muttered, "You're food's ready, did you want to go get it?"

"Oh, our food's ready, great!" The father replied without hearing all of my grumbling. That's okay though, I didn't really want to embarrass him in front of his kids. I'm not that cold. I was almost that cold as my jest was squashed before my eyes, but I held it back.

Within the same rush, a couple of ladies, that were part of the same wave of people, where getting upset because I hadn't just brought them their check (like I telepathically know that they wanted).

A couple ladies had ordered in the 'second tier', got their drinks and their food before I was at the end of my 'third tier' of order taking. I think they were pretty lucky, considering how fast they received everything. The two heavy set women tore through their burritos like a level four tornado rips through a thirty-year-old, rotten, water-soaked barn in the middle of the Midwest. There was nothing left but fragments of the paper plates with some shredded lettuce and beef debris scattered on the table and floor. Their forks were gone, possibly devoured in the storm. Oh, the humanity.

While I was in the middle of taking someone else's order at an adjacent table, I heard one of them interrupt, "Excuse me, we have a plane to catch!" (We all knew that was coming!) Also keep in mind that they have now been there for a total of about twenty minutes.

I returned to the computer with about five new tables of drink and food orders. I'd put money on the fact that these new orders that weren't even rung in yet probably were on the same flight as the large women. Seeing that the women wasted no time eating like they were served giant Twinkies, they figured that I could drop what I was doing to help them. Screw my other 15 tables, right?

I also had two credit cards to run for other 'first tier' people, and a reminder note to myself to print out three other tables' checks.

The two ladies waddled up to the server station and reaffirmed the fact that they will just not accept that there were other people there. I sighed to release a little anxiety, and find, amongst all the other paperwork before me, their ticket. This was probably the angriest I was all day long. That is, until this: Their total was $21.04. While I straitened up all of the other paperwork that I needed to prepare myself for the lion's den, also known as my station, I noticed that one of the ladies pulled out a twenty and a one-dollar bill and set it down on top of the server station area. In my astonishment, right in front of me, the other lady searched through her little change purse with her sausage-like fingers for (that's right, you guessed it!) four pennies. By this time, I had completely stopped what I was doing to just stand there and watch her do this. As soon as the last penny hit the countertop, I scooped them into my hand and gave them a very exuberant side pitch into the garbage can. The pennies made a loud noise bouncing around like they were ball bearings rattling around in a pressure cooker. I grabbed the receipt before she could turn around and said, "Hey, that's great! Did you ladies need your receipt at all?"

I got no response.

I always ask people if they want their receipts. One of my new favorite lines to say to people when I get stiffed, which at the airport happens quite a bit, is this, "Excuse me, would you like your receipt so you can write that off...somehow?"

That one is *usually* reserved for those extra special bastards that receives their dime change and will put it right in her or her pocket without hesitation. Man, that's cheap.

SHOW ME YOU CAN DO BETTER ~ AND THEN TELL ME I SUCK

You know, it's bad enough being a cheap person, but trying to make up for it in different ways just doesn't cut the mustard. I've had a couple tables before that I know the service, beverages, timing, food, and everything else were perfect, yet these people will leave only a note and run away quickly before you can encounter it, let alone read it.

The example I have for you reminds me of how childish people can be. This happened at the airport when it was only moderately busy. These people obviously weren't in a hurry because they wouldn't have bothered writing me a note, right? I saw them as they left and they were moving rather speedily for the door. In my hindsight, I realized the similarities between this type of people and small children that do something bad and then run away chanting, "You can't catch me!"

If someone left a note in place of a tip, it will usually say something stupid like this little gem I got:

"Hey waiter, here's your tip. Learn to be a better server. You suck! We waited forever for our food, and when you took the order you had to repeat everything that we said. Oh, 'chicken or beef', that's a good one!"

What? Couldn't you find a better scapegoat than that to be a cheap ass? I know it doesn't fit the 'time formula', but 'forever' in this case equaled about ten minutes. Repeating the order, what was I thinking? I sure as shit don't want to be accurate! I wonder if he has the same problems when talking to the drive through people too.

"Okay, that was two happy burgers, large happy fries, and a Coke, correct?"

"Why the hell do you have to repeat everything I just ordered? Didn't you hear me the first time!?" Now, that's a good one.

Thank God in heaven that I can laugh about it now, but I tell you what; if I found that guy in the concourse, he would have eaten that fucking napkin. Lucky bastard got away.

Behold ~ The Verbal Tip

Another thing that almost anyone in the hospitality industry can relate to are 'verbal tips'. Let me explain for those of you who don't. The verbal tip, simply put, is in exchange for a gratuity of monetary value, you get one of those affirmations that you can do the job you have, and you can do it well. For example, "Hey! You're a really great server! Thank you ever so much for taking care of us! You did a spectacular job! Keep up the good work! Okay?"

What The Hell Is Wrong With You!?

In the years, I've gotten used to the aura of the verbal tip. I have actually let out moans of exasperation before people even finish their first sentence of a verbal tip.

If you are going to be lucky enough to receive a verbal tip, it will usually come to you after the check has broken fifteen dollars a person, or the table has small children that have the tendency to get more food on the floor, than in their mouths. Coincidentally, you have to clean it up regardless. Once again, glorified busboy.

Once you know what's going on, if you are lucky enough to get a tip off of that table at all, it won't be much. There have been a couple exceptions, but when I say a couple, I mean two. I actually want to extrapolate this into my daily financial habits. I think I would like to start with my rent:

"Hey, you know, you've just done wonders with the upkeep of this house! The new washer's working great! The landscaping is beautiful! Could you grab me a soda? Great! Thanks!"…And then not pay rent.

Or better yet, my car payment, "You guys have been nothing short of spectacular sending me my bills on time like that! You even give me a little envelope to use too! Hey, the car is running great! Could you grab me a soda? Great! Thanks!" Let's see just how long it takes for the repossession people to come along.

I think you get my point!

What The Hell Is Wrong With You!?

Don't Be A Tip Tease ~ Tip Jokes

Something else that drives me to anger management classes is when people say jokes dealing with a server or bartender's tip. This happens on a day-to-day basis. It's appalling. Like I have mentioned before, it's not a good conversational tool between the tipper and the 'tipee'. Also, I find it incredibly rude when a customer makes light of my primary income. Some of the following are actual excerpts of what I now call 'tip jokes'. I think they could all be answered with the simple response, "Fuck You!"

- "...You'd better pour my drink strong! Your tip depends on it!"
- "...This guys on the ball! He's getting a tip for sure!!"
- (Soon after making a joke that you, the server, doesn't laugh at) "...You want a tip, don't you?"
- "...You'd better do (anything extraordinary that you normally wouldn't do)...if you want a tip."
- "...It's not like I'm going to tip you anyway." (What!?)
- "...Your tips would be better if you took off your shirt." (More so for the ladies, not me, I take off my shirt and people go blind.)
- "Obviously you don't want a tip, do you?"
- "Hey, what's this 'tip' line for on my credit card slip?"
- "Oh, I suppose you want a tip too."
- "You haven't blow your tip yet, I tell ya!" (Are you waiting and hoping for me to make a mistake so you can save a few bucks?)
- "...I guess we'd better give you a tip after all." (Jeez, sorry to disappoint you, what changed your mind?)
- "Whoops! There goes your tip!"

WHAT THE HELL IS WRONG WITH YOU!?

There are hundreds of these not so catchy one-liners that are just uncalled for, so please, if you don't have anything nice to say, then shut up.

'HOOK IT UP!'

As some of you know, we all have all fallen into this trap in the assumption that it would better our tip...once. If you haven't yet, let me tell you this: If anyone ever uses the term 'hook it up' in a sentence – know that you will not receive a good tip. They could be talking about the tip they plan to give you. Or they could be telling you to give free stuff away or make things bigger or stronger. Rest assured, there is no truth to the first sentence, even in repercussion of the second sentence.

When I first started bartending, I waited on a small group of people that seemed to be a group of coworkers. The ringleader of the group would order drinks almost faster than I could make them. They seemed like cool people so I didn't think anything badly the first time the ringleader said 'Don't worry bro – I'll hook you up!' He said this a few times, all in different ways. For instance, he also asked me to hook them up with drinks. I was young and needed the money (wait a minute) so I hooked them up. I took care of a round of drinks for them. I saved him almost $20 from his bill. I figured that he would in fact hook me up. This is how I learned what 'hook it up' *really* means. His bill was about $100 by the time they were done. He paid in cash. I remember it vividly; he tipped me three dollars.

* * *

So for everyone's future reference, if someone says 'hook it up' – steer clear! Even if they only say it for their better well-being, or your tip; it's in the cards that someone's going to get screwed. That someone is you.

What The Hell Is Wrong With You!?

General Public's Lack Of Knowledge

As hard as I am on everyone, I will always believe that there is a poor understanding of how the whole gratuity thing works. I have, for everyone's convenience (and value added) included a crude, yet effective tip chart at the beginning of this chapter. If the numbers you see seem high to you, then your tips seem low to us. In case you didn't know, it is customary to leave 15 to 20 percent of the check total as a gratuity. If you do not do this, then no longer wonder why you don't get good service on a repeat visit somewhere. A good rule of thumb is this:

- Great tippers are remembered forever and adored
- Good tippers are remembered
- Bad tippers are remembered, but not in a good way
- People that don't tip are never liked, and sometimes overlooked (Sad, but true)

If you are one of those people that are never liked, know that redemption awaits you. A good example to see if you are in this category follows. When you order $14 in drinks, pay with a twenty, and receive six ones back as your change, there's a reason behind it. Please don't be that guy that always asks, "Why did you give me six ones? I know I saw a bunch of fives in your cash drawer."

Nobody what's to be that guy.

WHAT THE HELL IS WRONG WITH YOU!?

WHY TIPPING MATTERS SO MUCH

I have to add in this part for all the people out there that don't understand the personal repercussions that I face as a stiffed restaurant employee. I also wanted to add this in for anyone that has never worked in a restaurant before and think that I'm just whining or begging for *more money*.

I will now bring up just a couple of the tax paying issues of a restaurant employee. I know that some of these attributes apply to all tipped positions – once again, you can write in your own in the margins.

Restaurant employees are demanded by the IRS to claim all of their tips as income. The taxes withheld by the IRS are then taken out of a check. In Arizona, and many other states, at a pay rate of a little over two dollars an hour; this usually leaves no money left on the check. It is usually required by a time clock or a computer system to enter in your claimed tips before you can leave. In some situations, tips are **automatically claimed for you based on sales**. Restaurant employees are not out to beat the system – at least I'm not. Here's what I am out to beat. When I get stiffed once or twice, sure, I get upset, but I can blow it off. When I get stiffed on a repeated basis, I lose more than just your tip. Due to you buying something, sales are recorded. Even though you didn't leave a tip, the computer will assume that you did. I then will pay taxes on money that I never received. Which in turn will eat away at my already insignificant little check.

Another way that stiffing hurts restaurant employees actually comes from other restaurant employees. At many restaurants and bars across the country, some non-tipped restaurant employees are indirectly tipped. This is called 'tipping out'. This is a mandatory function to pay workers that help the actual tipped employees. For instance, bussers, bar backs, service bartenders, and expediters are all examples of these. These employees are

What The Hell Is Wrong With You!?

tipped out, again, based on a percentage of server's sales. Bussers are usually tipped 2% to 3% of the server's sales. Service bartenders will take 1% to 2% of the server's sales. So if a server's sales for a shift is $980, and they have to tip out 3% to their busser and 1% to their bartender; they give away $39.20 of their hard earned money. Let's say that that same server is a decent server and usually makes 15% of their sales. They would make $147 before tipping out; afterwards, $107.80. Granted, with those numbers, it would be a fairly busy day and one hundred dollars isn't bad. This is where you come in. Giving away $40 dollars, even when it's justified is hard to do. But for every person that stiffs or tips poorly, it comes directly out of the leftover $107. I wish for everyone on the planet to understand how this is so truly upsetting.

So remember when you stiff someone, you are actually taking money away from them, not to mention the time wasted to help your sorry ass.

What The Hell Is Wrong With You!?

Confusion Adds To The Situation

Here are a couple of things that I believe the knowledge is there, but the follow through is mediocre. These few could be seen as lack of knowledge, but I would hope that most of the time, it's just accidentally neglected.

When someone goes to a bar and pays with a credit card, there will be a line for a tip, then a blank line for the total, and then a third line for you to sign. People will, usually in the midst of a conversation with someone else, sign the bottom of the credit card slip and walk away. I get upset because there's nothing I can legally do in this situation. It has happened with small tabs and large tabs alike. I guess I could be a dishonest person and just write in whatever tip I feel I deserve, however, I'm not a fan of prison.

For any of you that do this, or know someone that does, I have heard a rebuttal to my dispute. Some people have told me that maybe they think the tip is already included. If that were the case, why would the tip line be there? Let me go a little further. Do you sign a blank income tax form and just assume that someone else has done it correctly? This is your money, man!

I hear that in a large majority of countries, the gratuity is automatically added in to every check. Not here. The majority of bars and restaurants in America will **not** add the tip to your bill. The only exception to this rule is if you have a large party of people. Usually you will need more than eight people for this. Even then, sometimes it is not added in the hopes that the server will receive more then the 15 percent 'autograt'. Please, read everything you put your signature on. You never know; if I become bitter enough, when I see you at the bar, I might just have you sign over power of attorney while you argue with someone on your cell phone. Hey, that's a great idea.

What The Hell Is Wrong With You!?

Don't Try To Split Your Check If You Lack Skills In Math

Even though this one makes me want to strangle people, I have to understand that this could just be something overlooked. I want to bring this to the world's attention, because I'm the one getting screwed.

This is an actual situation that happened quite recently. I had a rather large table, but not large enough to add in the tip. It was about six people. When they were all finished, their tab equaled $73. As a normal feeling of mine, I do not like splitting up checks. No one does. However, I will go that extra mile to avoid this; or not to give anyone the opportunity to short my tab on a technicality. The people decided to split up the check on their own. Usually when this happens, they forget a soda or drink here and there, or they will forget about the tax all together. This further sucks money out of any tip that's left. But those are things that can be discussed comfortably. What I'm getting at is much more disturbing.

After they split everyone's total off of the check, they hand me a stack of cash, and a credit card. Every time I see this, I become discouraged. I know that the chances of getting screwed are very good at this point. They seal my financial coffin when they say, "Okay, take off the money and put the remainder on the credit card."

At this moment, I want to say something. To this day, I can't think of a delicate way to put it. Here's what happens. I will take out the cash from the total. In this situation, they gave me $42 in cash. This made their total only $31. They then tipped me on the $31. Granted, they tipped me 20%, but on less then half of their bill. I made $6 on that table. A table that actually took up *two* tables and occupied those tables for quite some time. A little quick math for you, that wound up being 8%. Like I said before, I

What The Hell Is Wrong With You!?

believe that it's just an oversight. Here is my message to the world. I believe that the person with the credit card needs to take control of the situation. You are the treasurer! Make sure that this travesty stops here and now. God bless you treasurer!

It's All About Real Estate

Here is one that makes me wonder if anybody ever notices his or her surroundings anymore. It almost sounds like a joke to me. A guy walks into a restaurant. He sits down and orders a $7 lunch. The restaurant gets really busy. He finishes his lunch, moves his plate aside and demands a refill. Meanwhile, his server is contemplating how great it would be to have that table that seats five people to be available for all the people waiting at the front door. The guy moves to the sports section of the local newspaper, then the business section, then the comics, then the horoscopes, then the obituaries, what have you. He smokes a cigarette, or a pack of cigarettes. When the lunch rush dies down, he realizes that it's time for him to go back to work. He throws a dollar on the table and leaves.

I know, it's not funny, it's not supposed to be. I have no problem with someone going to a restaurant during his or her lunch break and reading, say, *War And Peace*. But if you are by yourself, sit at a smaller table, or sit at the bar. If you really have that much time in your lunch break, go home.

I'm very insistent on this issue because God only knows what money I could have made on that table. Just say it was sat and cleaned four times in that one rush; that would equal around $20 to $25. I want to point out that a big part of this business deals with real estate. I ask the world to be conscientious on this fact. We like to make money at work and if we can't, it's upsetting.

What The Hell Is Wrong With You!?

Water Drinkers

A big one on tipping deals with the actual meaning of the word. A tip is a 'present of money to someone for some service'. It would be easily thought out that if the service were decreased, the present of money would be equally decreased. I agree with that - it's basic logic. However, many people seem to forget logic when it goes the other way. If you receive a great deal of service, the present of money should increase proportionately.

For instance, if there is a party of six people and they want to save a little money, they will order six waters (with extra lemon so they can make their own lemonade!). They don't have to pay the price of the sodas which could vary anywhere between $6 and $13.50, depending on where you are. Now, first off, the server will be hurt a little because, tipping on a percentage, the bill will be smaller, and so will the tip. Here's where it gets aggravating. **It should be taken into consideration that your server took a whole lot of time to get your 437 water refills during your lunch!** Please keep this in mind. Tip accordingly.

Discounts And Coupons

No tipped employee likes to see coupons and/or discounts in this business. I understand that both are marketing devices used to increase the restaurant or bar's sales (in the long run) and promote repeat business. I completely agree with the use of these tools. However, from a tipped employee's view and due to the actions of the general public, there are deplorable issues.

Most people, it troubles me to say, will use these discounts and then tip on the percentage of the final cost. For instance, two people come in to a restaurant and order two meals, one for $8 and one for $7. There total would have been $15, but they have a coupon for one free meal. There total is now only $8 (not including tax in the equation). We'll assume that the people are decent 17% tippers. Instead of receiving $2.55, I would only receive $1.36. My service was the same, the food they received was the same, the table was just like all the others; but my tip was damn near chopped in half. Why?

I think this one really shows that people can be good tippers, but a little too frugal. Even though they still tipped me, I'll clue you in to a little something extra. Contrary, no, non-existent to popular belief, even though you had a coupon and didn't have to pay for a meal, the sales were still reported under my social security number in the paperwork of the restaurant. It's still a sale, and along with what I said a few pages ago, I will still be liable for reporting and being taxed on the tips that I never received.

If you are one of these people, please keep this in mind and understand why at some places the server will show you the **total before discount**. This is what you tip on. That's why it's there!

If You Want Someone To Sing 'Happy Birthday' To You ~ Grab The Phone Book, Look Up Telegram-Singing

Something I feel I must talk about is not to expect singing from your server. I have worked in many restaurants where the employees have all gotten together to sing happy birthday to embarrass the hell out of a guest. I actually find it more embarrassing to me. Actually, I think is belittling. The guest can order another beer, while I can't even have one to sooth my nerves. I actually think that the other guests in the restaurant are agitated by the entire episode as well. This is a true story. Once, due to being *dragged* into singing at someone else's table, another customer voiced his opinion. When the server of that table announced, "May I have your attention please, tonight is Chris' twenty-third birthday…"

What The Hell Is Wrong With You!?

The customer from the back of the restaurant broke the uncomfortable silence with, "Who cares!"

* * *

If you do go to a restaurant that you know sings happy birthday, please notice what's going on around you before you ask. For instance, if it's noon on a Friday, it's probably not a good idea to ask for everyone to stop what they're doing to sing you a song. Most restaurants will be so busy on a Friday lunch that every employee will be sprinting through the restaurant, or at least power walking. Nothing should interfere with the semi-smooth workings of a Friday lunch. It's just like the idiot who will fill out a job application and then call back during a lunch period. Rest assured, your message is delivered to the manager with a small addition – don't hire this idiot.

Most of us know of at least two of these places where the song is sang in a festive and fitting way. Don't go to just any restaurant and <u>expect</u> this to happen. In the past, I would hide in the walk-in cooler stocking beer or something when I was called to sing. I know that's not being part of the team, but guess what, it wasn't in my contract.

There was this one time in particular where a table of three people expected this singing from me. It was busy that night and nearing the end of the dinner rush. I walked up to the table to bus their dirty dishes away. One of them looked up at me while pointing to his buddy and said, "Hey, it's this guy's birthday!"

"Hey, wonderful, happy birthday, guy!" I responded.

"Well…aren't you going to sing happy birthday?" He looked up at me like I should have just burst into song for their table all by myself. At this place, it was not required to sing happy birthday, thank God.

"Actually, no, I don't sing happy birthday to my tables, sorry to disappoint you." I replied smiling because, at that time, I was remembering my old jobs where I had.

145

WHAT THE HELL IS WRONG WITH YOU!?

"Oh, okay, well does he get anything for free?" Don't tell me you didn't see that one coming.

"I can get him a birthday shot from the bar if he wants." I said. Evidentially, as the birthday boy shook his head no, he didn't seem to want one. I told them okay, smiled, nodded my head and continued to bus their table. When I returned to the table I saw my manager standing next to the table apologizing for the **bad service**. I overheard the guy saying that they come in all the time and have never had such horrible service before. Of course, none of my other tables seemed to have a problem, however, none of them wanted me to sing. The manager then took care of the entire bill, that's right, everything consumed. I didn't get a tip, but the manager did question me. After telling him what had really happened, he told me not to worry, they were probably just after something for free.

On a side note, I have actually run into this when I was a manager. I learned that buying people's food after they have eaten everything isn't always such a good idea. It yields many scams. Don't get me wrong, I still have a few ounces of customer satisfaction in me, but if they ate all the food, there must not have been too much of a problem. I will use my personal experiences later in chapter 17 – 'A Gutsy Way To Dine And Dash?'

* * *

One other thing; if you want a free meal on your birthday, go to Denny's, or find some real friends.

WHAT THE HELL IS WRONG WITH YOU!?

THE TALE OF MR. FOURSTAR...AT THE AIRPORT

Every once in a while I will run into people who just don't realize their surroundings. This time, I'm not necessarily talking about how busy a place is, but the actual place itself. This happens in great numbers at the airport. These are the people that always think that they are in a four star restaurant. I know the attitude as soon as I see their pretentious swagger through the door. It makes me sick. I know the type all to well. I remember them from when I worked in fine dining at a restaurant on the outskirts of a popular Phoenix resort. The restaurant was actually about three blocks away. Most of our clientele were the people from the surrounding business area. Even though their bills were only about $10 a person, they expected the same service that you would find from the expensive restaurants up 'on top of the hill' so to speak. Some average lower working-class people would come in to pretend that they could boss us around like the pompous idiots that spend a couple thousand dollars a stay just down the road.

However, when you are at the airport, you do have to be polite and hospitable, but you do not have to kiss everyone's ass to keep your job. A good example of what I mean comes to us from the middle of the bar.

He didn't necessarily dress the type so it was hard for me to understand exactly where he was coming from at first. I remember that the other bartender working with me had just taken a break. I was all by myself. As most of you that work in restaurants know, once you are by yourself, or order food for yourself, it will get busy. I don't know why or how, but in never fails. It's Murphy's Law. I had seven new people all sit down at the bar and simultaneously the printer for the server's drinks went nuts with orders. As I said before, my first priority is always to get something in front of every person so they don't wait empty-handed. As quickly as I could, I got all the drinks for the seven people sitting at the bar. The man in question, we will call Mr. Fourstar. I'm sure he could feel the anxiousness in my voice as I asked him what he wanted to drink. He went through the whole 'what do have on tap' game, then decided on one.

"Would you like a large draft?" I hurried.

"Okay, that sounds good." He responded.

"If you want, I can get you a shot of anything for two dollars." I said not wasting any time.

"That sounds good, get me a shot of Belvedere (vodka)." He replied.

I don't understand why Mr. Fourstar didn't see right away that he wasn't in a high-class restaurant. I mean what kind of high-class joint would offer a shot for two dollars, but maybe he goes to those budget resorts. I know what you're thinking, and no, I've never heard of one either.

I continued on. Once all of the new people had obtained their drinks, I went to the service well. I took care of those eight or so drinks for the servers and then went back to the people at the bar. I asked everyone in succession if everything was okay. A slow thinking monkey could have been able to tell that I was as busy as a day care attendant whose kids had just found the candy stash. When I got to the sixth person at the bar, Mr. Fourstar had a devilish little grin on his fat little face. He had a menu lying on the bar in front of him.

"Can I get you something to eat?" I questioned, now with less haste.

"No, actually, I'm just waiting for the chips and salsa service." He said without changing the smirk on his face. The man next to him started to laugh *at* him. I actually thought he was laughing with Mr. Fourstar at first and expected free chips and salsa himself.

WHAT THE HELL IS WRONG WITH YOU!?

I know that most to all sit-down Mexican restaurants do give out free chips and salsa to every patron. This wasn't the whole problem. This was just one small aspect to his eccentricity. Basically, what bothers me is that if you are in a place that serves three-dollar meals from the fast food joint next door on Styrofoam plates and plastic silverware, chips and salsa service will not be in your immediate future.

In traumatic disbelief that he would say something like that **at the airport**, I responded, "Actually, you have to order food to receive it here." I pointed out 'Chips and Salsa' on the menu laying in front of him that he didn't feel the need to read. This is where it all began to make sense to me. The next line uttered from Mr. Fourstar's poor misguided mouth told me why he was having such a problem.

"Well, I would suppose so. I'd expect that from a place that doesn't even chill my shot of vodka for me." His smirk soon dropped to a pout.

"Did you ask me to chill it?" I returned reprehensibly.

"I shouldn't have to, that's the way it *should* be served." He said back to me in a snooty tone.

You know, I've only been a bartender for five years, so maybe I'm not a *professional*. I have learned that everyone has different opinions on how they like their alcohol. God knows just as well as you do that if I *did* chill every shot that I made, most of the people would complain.

"Well, here you just have to ask for what you want, or you won't get what you want." I said back as I walked away thinking how terrible my job would be if I did have to chill every single liquor shot, for two dollars, at the airport. I would never get anything done!

I was kind of upset at how he said those things, yet still laughing because maybe, just maybe, Mr. Fourstar had been joking the whole time. Nobody could be that serious at the airport, right?

What The Hell Is Wrong With You!?

About ten minutes goes by and the manager on duty, Jan, walks behind the bar. Jan is one of my favorite managers of all times because she talks shit to the customers just like I do. She does though care more about satisfaction than I do. She also gives me a great deal of shit too.

Jan coincidentally walked up to the guy at the bar. I was hoping that she would shove her size ten and a half all up his ass. Instead, she opened with, "Is everything okay here?" Pointing up at me in a joking manner (unlike one found in a fine dining establishment), "Is this guy giving you a hard time?" I looked over to notice that Mr. Fourstar, with the floodgates opened, started to complain about not getting free chips and salsa. At first, I thought he could still be joking and was playing around with Jan too. Then I realized, soon after Jan realized, that Mr. Fourstar was actually complaining about not getting **free food**. My chuckles reverted to the standard churns of anger that I was used to with these kinds of people.

"...And that guy over there," Mr. Fourstar said pointing at me, "didn't even chill my shot of vodka!"

"Did you ask for your shot to be chilled?" Jan asked in a more sincere tone than before. Now that two people have asked Mr. Fourstar if he let me know in the first place, he should've figured it out. He didn't.

"Well, no, but I shouldn't have to." Mr. Fourstar said like a spoiled twelve-year-old girl trying to reconcile a wrongdoing. You just wanted to smack him in the head.

"You know, he isn't going to know what you want unless you tell him," I could tell that Jan had switched to full customer service mode. After a long silent pause from Mr. Fourstar, Jan continued, "I'll tell you what I'm going to do."

Shocked as I watched, Jan took care of Mr. Fourstar's tab. I was a little irked because he didn't have one legitimate complaint. Then I was livid because Mr. Fourstar gave me a childish little leer as if to say 'Mom likes me better'. Now I wanted to punch him.

Jan then told me that he seemed upset and she took care of the tab so the other bartender and I could get a tip. I figured as much anyway, but a big part of me wouldn't have given him <u>anything</u> for free! I would have charged him double! I was bitter. His tab was just under $20 when Jan took care of it. Mr. Fourstar soon left after this, probably because there's little chance of getting anything else for free.

I walked over to see what kind of tip he left. As I walked down the bar, I remember back to the tipping behavior of the people at that so called 'fine dining' Mexican restaurant by that resort. It shows the common ingredients to making an idiot like this certain breed of people. Most of these people will expect perfect service and tip poorly if the littlest thing goes awry. These are the type of people that will order an iced tea without lemon. Due to the force of habit, a lemon will make its way onto the rim of the cup. This person will take off the lemon, showing he's not allergic, and throw it across the table like you just keyed his car (That was, by the way, a true account). I wouldn't be surprised if I heard a story of these people not leaving a tip because the interior decorating in the restaurant wasn't Feng Shui and the energy didn't feel right. Like I said before, if a tab came to $30 to $40 for three people including drinks from before, my history proves that their tip left would be $3 to $4. It would lead you to believe that since you *thought* you were in a fine dining restaurant, you should have enough forethought to leave a fine dining restaurant tip; instead of tipping like you were at a Jaybeez family restaurant!

Anyhow, I got to the middle of the bar where Mr. Fourstar was sitting. Two dollars. He got everything for free, and left two dollars. Even if he had to pay for everything that he got, two dollars would still be a punch to the gut. This is especially bad because, again, it's split between two people. So essentially, I made a dollar. Sure, I understand, one dollar is still money. All I need is two hundred seventy eight more people like that, and it's a car payment! It could add up, but in the mean time, it just pisses me off. I guess I could make a phone call with that 10-10-whatever thing.

Moral of the story: If you are at a bar or restaurant, and nothing is wrong, but you get things for free, chances are it's so you will leave a good tip. There are a couple of exceptions to the rule due to sympathy. If you're a hard luck case at the time, the bartender's just trying to save you a few bucks. In any other case, the bartender wants the few bucks. Duh.

* * *

I'm terribly sorry if this chapter seemed like venting…it was! I encourage the people that whom haven't worked in a restaurant to read it. If you are one of those people that throw in an extra quarter on top of the seventeen cents you had already left me to see if my dropped jaw will close, this could help you. You couldn't even imagine some of the things said about you; sometimes in a conversation right in front of you. These nuances can be found by anyone if you look hard enough. However, they are not rare to me; I've seen them for many years. Trust me, you don't want to be that guy, either.

* * *

Just so you know as well, there have been many times that I've received a bad tip and deserved it. None of those times were mentioned here. I actually could double the size of this chapter with stories like that. There have been countless times that I've been too tired, or too sick, too sick and tired, or too hungover to work efficiently. It goes with the territory; everyone in this business can relate. All of those bad tips are justified. Even though I will still tip well on bad service, I can't expect the rest of the world to. Just please don't expect the world in a hand basket unless you are in a place that obviously serves it.

WHAT THE HELL IS WRONG WITH YOU!?

Also, I know what some of you are probably thinking, too. Maybe I just really suck. It could be a perception of some people, but I think that I do very well. I know that I'm a good bartender. I don't think I'm the greatest server in the world, but it's my own fault. I get so damn pissed off at people, more so when I serve, I lose my train of thought. It's a problem I know I have with my anger management. That's probably why this book wound up being so long. Get out my aggression before I crack for good. On the other side of the coin, if you are reading this and don't know me, I probably won't *be able* to find another job in a restaurant – ever again. I guess I better learn how to drive a truck.

What The Hell Is Wrong With You!?

Chapter Numero Doce – Fake ID's

Everyone who has been in this industry has seen fake ID's. Whether or not you have fallen for them, God only knows. Some that I've seen through training, I wouldn't even second-guess them as being authentic.

I'm not going to get into a big chapter on how to spot fake ID's. You should know to check typeface, see if the picture looks like the person, or if they needed to dig it out of a dark, secretive inset in the bowels of one's bag or wallet, what have you. It's a really good thing to be careful. Cops do send in underage kids into bars (and stores) to bust people for serving them. In Arizona, they're called 'shrills'. What worries me the most is that in this state, the person that *serves* the underage person could go to jail and receive thousand dollar fines. Like I said about the credit card issue in the last chapter, I'm still not a big fan of prison.

The fake ID's that kids spend time and effort on will immediately be known as fake, or they will be served – depending on one's talent. Don't feel bad if you do sometimes serve them because minors will always be drinking in bars, one way or another; it's inevitable. I'm sure that everyone reading this has before, or, hell, is now.

* * *

I have seen old laminated ID's that have been split apart, another photo added on top of the existing photo, and then ironed back together. I don't see how people think that I'm not going to be able to tell that the picture is three times thicker than the rest of the license.

One of my friends told me about one of the best fake ID's he'd ever seen. Someone made a real cheesy ID card like the newer plastic credit card style licenses. To emulate a magnetic strip on the back, they had simply put on a strip of black electrical

154

tape. Like that's really pulling the wool over someone's eyes, I'm sure.

I've seen all kinds from scratched out dates, faded photos to poorly adjusted dates like they just used a typewriter (i.e. instead of 1974, it would say 19**74**).

* * *

Now then, this chapter is just a short story that happened to me. I would never believe some of these things if it didn't happen to me.

The best situation that I've ever run across was with a younger traveler at the airport. A younger, pudgy, Mexican kid comes in and sits down in my section. One of the best things about working at the airport is that everyone needs a picture ID to board the airplane. Here, I don't have to hear all the lame excuses like 'come on dude, I'm 21!'

I walked over to him and asked if he wanted something to drink.

"Yeah man, gimme one of those big Buds." He asked with a big smile on his face.

"Okay, can I see your ID?" I asked.

"Sure man!" He exclaimed proudly as he handed me the ID. I took a look at it and at the very first glance I started to laugh. His grin quickly shrank to a disappointed frown. I still couldn't believe what I was looking at. It was a California ID with a picture of a 21-year-old kid that was 125 pounds, blonde, and whiter than snow.

"Uh, this is you?" I asked, still laughing.

"Yeah."

"Okay, do you have something else in your wallet with your name on it?" A good one to ask if an ID is questionable.

"Nope, just my ID."

"Okay, what's your address?" There was a long pause for him to think about where *he* lived.

What The Hell Is Wrong With You!?

"1827 north Madison?" He said, or more so questioned.

"Nope, try again." I figured I'd have some fun with him.

"1287 north Madison." He said, with a little more confidence.

"No, I'm afraid you just moved yourself about four blocks down the road." I apologized and told him that I couldn't serve him. His smile returned and he left the bar. I may have been a little harsh, I suppose, if he was a dyslexic, weight gaining white guy with a really, really dark tan. If that was the case, I apologize, but I'm pretty sure I was right on that one.

I Need An ID When I Go To A Bar?

Something that I love about this job and being able to ask to see someone's ID is listening to all the excuses for the lack of license. I've added a small list of some of the few funnier ones I've heard. I'm sure you could add in more.

- ❑ I left it in my other pants
- ❑ It's out in my car (go get it!)
- ❑ My dog ate it
- ❑ The cops have it from a DUI (oh, okay – you driving?)
- ❑ I don't have one
- ❑ I'm 21; don't you believe me?
- ❑ (My favorite:) I just got a new wallet and I haven't switched everything over yet. (Who's that lazy!?)

WHAT THE HELL IS WRONG WITH YOU!?

BASIC 'DON'TS' WHEN YOU ARE OUT AT THE BAR

When people ask me for a Corona, 75% of those people will feel the need to remind me that it comes with a lime. I know it comes with a lime. We all know it comes with a lime. It's on every commercial, poster, and blow-up plastic promotion bottle. People saying stupid things like this are pet peeves of mine that ranks up there with the people who own huge, jacked up, four-by-four SUVs that are designed to travel rough terrain and take driveways at two and a half miles an hour. There is no need to ask anymore. Please stop.

The next chapters are for every other little note, like the one above. These chapters are dedicated to all the stupid people that 'make it happen' on a day-to-day basis. For instance, where else could you go, but to a bar, where you can walk into an empty restroom to find the sinks just running away? Most of these things are pet peeves of restaurant workers. Even though, we can all laugh at the things here, we still get irked every time they happen. I encourage all of you again to use this as a quick reference guide for the customers that do these things to better themselves, and the world.

What The Hell Is Wrong With You!?

Chapter Numero Trece: Terms Of Endearment

This is going to be the most important piece of advice that you can ever have if you want to keep the bartender or server on your good side. Here are a few examples of pet names you should NEVER USE when someone is serving you:

- ✓ Pal, or any variation of the root like Pally
- ✓ Sweetheart, Hon, Honey, Babe; a girl saying this is a-okay, but when a guy says it, it's wrong…especially to another guy
- ✓ Son, Boy, or Kid; the only exception is if you are actually that person's legal parent or guardian
- ✓ Skip, or any variation of the root like Skippy, or Skipper
- ✓ Hey You! It makes a great Pink Floyd song, it also makes you wait longer
- ✓ Cowboy; if you work in a country bar, you won't ever get away from that – I'm sorry.
- ✓ Any of the Jerky Boy's nicknames like Fruitcake; actual sentence used by my customer, "Hey, fruitcake, make that drink a double!" You could guess that I was sure to pour extra.
- ✓ Killer; unless you want it to come true
- ✓ Any adjective followed by the ending '-stuff'; for instance hot stuff, good stuff, fuck stuff, etc.
- ✓ Dickhead; this actually happened to a bartender at the airport in my presence.
- ✓ Bar Bitch; I personally hate this one, some of the girls I know in the business sometimes like it. You know who you are.

What The Hell Is Wrong With You!?

- ✓ Chief; fire fighters and cops wouldn't call me chief, why is it okay if you're a retard? I usually respond with, "Yes Indian?"
- ✓ Beerman; it was cute in the commercial, the first time
- ✓ Sport, or any variation of the root like Sport-o or Sporty
- ✓ Toots, or any variation of the root like Tootsy
- ✓ Buddy; unless I am your buddy
- ✓ Young fellow; it's just nerve-racking
- ✓ Dude; at most times will be found as inappropriate
- ✓ Big guy; acceptable if I were a 2-year-old that hadn't pooped himself
- ✓ Any others I've left out, feel free to use the margins

If you have worked in a bar for more than three days, I'm sure you could fill up at least another page. There is one exception to the whole 'name game' when it comes to me. If you are a woman, preferably attractive, you can and will get away with calling me most of the names above. I would, however, still veer away from the ones like Dickhead, Fruitcake, and Bar Bitch; that will just hurt me.

* * *

For everyone else out there, there are names that you can use without pissing off too many people. I will list some of the better ways to get the attention of your bartender. These should clear up any problems.

- ✓ Bartender
- ✓ Barkeep
- ✓ Partner (at times!)
- ✓ Sir
- ✓ You can also just ask for something as the person walks by; no bartender or server could really get mad at that.
- ✓ 'Excuse me', said in a reasonable tone

WHAT THE HELL IS WRONG WITH YOU!?

- ✓ Nonchalantly hold your money out in front of you like a flag; no need to wave it around, we can smell it
- ✓ (The best one) Sit on your happy ass and wait to be served.

If you wait more than ten minutes (that's twenty five minutes for those of you using the formula from chapter six) then you should say something. It may be a dead giveaway that you could be in a really busy atmosphere and just not know you are.

WHAT THE HELL IS WRONG WITH YOU!?

CHAPTER NUMERO CATORCE: WHISTLING, SNAPPING, AND OTHER SPASTIC MOVES

It's a fact that if you are a whistler or a snapper, you are just telling the world that you like to wait for a long time when you go out. Don't ever do that. Especially those gifted with the ability to stick your dirty little fingers in your mouth and whistle so loud that dogs can hear you two blocks away. That's a great little trick you can do there, but it's like your car horn; use it for salutations and emergencies. That's it! Here is another thing to keep in mind if you are one of these people. When our back is turned to you as you whistle and snap at us over and over again, it's pretty safe to ascertain that we hear you all right; we're just ignoring you. I can't stress on this enough; there is no 'quick service' award for the loudest bar heckler!

* * *

Another ghastly deed to avoid is the episodes of frantic waving to get your server or bartender's attention. I've seen people do this almost immediately after they sit down <u>as I talk to a different table</u>. How rude! If you are a 'waver', please keep in mind that your server or bartender may just be a hospitable and/or a personable person. Also keep in mind that, chances are, you are not the only one in the bar or restaurant. You wave like that; it's just guaranteeing yourself that no one will be with you anytime soon.

Again, like whistling, there are no extra points for intensity. The little puppy dog paw on the car's side window routine, all the way to the seizure-like eruptions of arm waving like you're stranded on a desert island and just saw an airplane.

I'm just baffled on the amount of people in this world that think they'll be served first because they flail their arms around like an excited monkey. Please take note that if you are in a busy restaurant or bar and you start flapping them around, your server is

WHAT THE HELL IS WRONG WITH YOU!?

not going to drop what their doing and run right over to assist you. As a matter of fact, little distractions like that could throw off a server's entire train of thought! I know it does for me; because instead of thinking about the 38 things I need to do immediately, I'm thinking of nothing but smacking you out of your tantrum! Yes, I'm bitter! I'll tell you why.

* * *

This is one of my favorite stories on the subject. It happened to me when I was serving in the sports bar called McDuffy's. It was a busy football game-day at home where the Arizona Cardinals' stadium sits about four blocks away. We were exceedingly busy after the game. As soon as people would get up and leave their tables, new people would sit down before I could clean them up. I was taking an order at an adjacent table when this very thing happened.

Four people at the booth behind me got up and left. Five new people promptly sat down. In front of them remained the empty pitchers, glasses, dirty napkins, plates, etc. As I was asking a customer at the adjacent table if they wanted fries, coleslaw, cottage cheese, or a salad with his burger, I heard a subtle "Psst." I was taking an order with someone else, so I chose to ignore it. No more than thirty seconds later, I heard it again, "Psssst." This time, however, it was a little louder and longer in duration. Again, I chose to ignore it. It's just rude to the table I was at.

They say that the third time's a charm. With a lessened pause than before, having a crescendo like a full orchestra, and long enough for me to cut them off, I heard, "Psssssss…"

"What could possibly be so important that you need to interrupt me when I'm talking to another table!?" I exclaimed after I broke and turned around from the original table mid-sentence.

What The Hell Is Wrong With You!?

"Oh, well, I just wanted to see if you could clear off this table for us?" The lady replied, slowly sinking her level back down to the subtleties of the first 'Psst'.

"Yeah, I will. It's part of my job. But you sat down at a dirty table no more than <u>one minute ago</u>, may I finish taking this table's order?" I asked as I pointed down to the original table.

"Oh, okay, sure, go ahead."

"Thank you…shit." I said.

Moral of the story: If you choose to sit at a dirty table, here is your warning. You might have to sit at that dirty table until it is cleaned. I know that makes so much sense that it's hard to figure out. Just don't think too hard; your head will explode.

What The Hell Is Wrong With You!?

Chapter Numero Quince: If You Think You're Really Funny, You're Probably Not

We usually find this person saying all the tip jokes similar to the ones mentioned in chapter eleven. They will also be accompanied by a bunch of really bad and/or inappropriate jokes. This person is usually easily found. After he says one of these so-called banters, he will laugh boisterously for a short moment of time, and then look around at all the people that simultaneously sigh at his presence – and then continue to laugh boisterously. He never stops. He will still think that he is the most hysterical person on the planet and he won't give up until last call. I'll give you a few examples to pinpoint these people.

A good example of this happened just tonight at the bar. This guy was sitting at the bar trying very hard to flirt with the woman next to him. He would voice his opinion about everything. I asked the girl next to him if she wanted another drink. She hesitated for a little while, and then asked me for a small one.

"It's 4:05 right now and your flight boards at 4:15," he jested, "and you want another beer? Come on! Wha ha ha ha ha!"

I can't say anything bad about the statement itself because it was the truth, but it wasn't funny. The thing is him laughing about it so audibly it rings throughout the bar, and he can't stop laughing through the first, second, **third, or fourth time saying the same damn thing verbatim**, it gets annoying.

Luckily for me, this same person stuck around to pester me further. My anger level continued to grow as this guy over exaggerated an already trying situation.

I'm not really sure why, but tonight was a strange night at the airport. It was really slow all night long except for the last hour and a half. During this time, like any rush at the airport, we would start running out of everything. Being instantly busy, we all became flustered and frustrated. Bombarded by dirty glassware that needed to be washed, mounds of people all waiting to order, or waiting for drinks, and then a keg blows (empties), the last thing you need is *this guy*.

"Whoops!! Looks like you've got yourself a little problem! Wha ha ha ha ha!"

Is this necessary!? Nobody else is laughing with you! Look around you! For some reason, again, he will repeat himself over and over again, saying the same stupid and causeless phrase. He will also be looking around at the other people that aren't laughing like he's trying to *get them* to laugh. Trying to comprehend the logic that could possibly be thought by this person to make it acceptable is enough to send me right into a panic attack. Stop it! You're not funny! Ask around!

* * *

A bartender usually easily ignores these people. A good way to tell is when the bartender listens to your story and just smiles and nods his or her head. If hospitality industry workers are even remotely interested in your story, then they will usually throw in their two cents worth; it's part of the job.

Additionally, sometimes these people will say something so horrible, so dastardly that no one will want to listen to them anymore. They may even do things to help everyone ignore them. For instance, turn up the radio or television, change subjects, or just walk away.

I once had to change the subject to try to shut a certain guy up. This guy somehow managed to use the words 'slut' and 'whore' in every sentence he said. If he were by himself, where no one could hear him, it would be okay – like a sanitarium. Seeing that there was a bar full of people including three really attractive women *right next to him*, it was not called for. The guy never caught on to me trying to change the subject to things where you couldn't use words like that like mom, church, food…nothing

WHAT THE HELL IS WRONG WITH YOU!?

worked. The three women then scolded him in a very sassy way as he 'talked to the palms of their hands'. I tried to help, that's what I'm here for.

What The Hell Is Wrong With You!?

Chapter Numero Dieciseis: Will The Real White Rapper Guy Please Stand Up?

I'm not going to bring up any of my opinions about the music industry these days. I will say that I'm happy for all the people that have made it out there. Some of their fans, however, create a different story. I think it's cool to have role models in life to help you do the things that you want to do, but there should be some kind of limitations on this. For instance, I admire Jerry Cantrel, the guitarist from Alice In Chains; therefore, I play guitar. I think magic shows are pretty cool, but I'm not about grow out my hair, wear tight leather pants, stand a friend up against a door and through knives at his head. The point I'm trying to make is that if you are a rap star, you can fit the rap star motif. If not, feel free to enjoy what you listen to, but please don't try so hard to *be* that person. Especially if you look like me (see back cover).

This story is added in to try to demonstrate how some of Americas' youth is. These people are usually found in certain demographics. They will be Caucasian, 16 to about 23, and will usually have rich parents that show an obvious lack of discipline.

This person in particular was a small-framed pale white boy. He dressed in droopy white pants, a white sleeveless shirt, backwards white baseball cap, and hanging just off his shoulders – a big ass white coat like he was in the artic circle. (Who's that remind you of?) The coat really threw me for a loop because it was the middle of the summer. The bar that I work in at the airport is in a concourse with no international flights. Where was he going that he needed that big ass coat? I mean he must have been suffering in that coat, just to look good. No wonder he was so gaunt; it's his own little portable sauna. Anyhow, I understand that it's a style, and even if I don't like it, I can accept it. That wasn't the problem; it was the attitude:

WHAT THE HELL IS WRONG WITH YOU!?

"Can I get you something to drink?" I asked even though I knew he wasn't old enough to stay in the bar by himself; I started in a polite and professional way.

"No, I'm just going to smoke a cigarette." He said in a cocky tone.

"Okay, that's cool, can I see your ID?" I asked.

"Why, to smoke a cigarette?"

"Yep! In Arizona, you have to be 21 to be in a bar. Are you 21?"

"No, but it doesn't matter because I'm going to sit here anyway." He replied with a mad-dog voice. Like I've said before, when my tables are being taken up, I'm not making any money. He had to go.

"Actually, buddy, you do have to leave."

"Look, I'm going to sit here as long as I want and smoke. So step off." He said back as the obvious tough-guy rebellion started to shine.

"There's two ways we can do this," I explained to him, "either you can put out your cigarette and leave, or I can call the cops (on bicycles) and have them do it for you. You do know that cops in this airport are about thirty seconds away, right?"

"Fine." He said with frustrating withdraw. He extinguished his cigarette, and walked out the door.

WHAT THE HELL IS WRONG WITH YOU!?

I really don't understand that attitude at all. I'm sure it's just a phase, but if not, his actions should have been different. If he was really *keeping it real*, I think he should have waited for the man, got kicked out of the bar, and missed his flight – all for the sake of his standoffishness with me. I'm not trying to be vindictive (this time). I just wanted to see if he could get on the airport intercom and start busting out a dope rhyme about the oppression at the airport. Hey! Maybe I'm on to something here. Check it! Check it!

The Man Forced Me,
Little Rapper Wannabe,
To Uphold The Law,
While Everyone Saw!
Word.

Yeah, that sucks. *My bad.*

By the way, for all of the others like the description above; how can you people walk around outside in winter ware in Phoenix, Arizona? It's like 120 degrees outside! I don't care who you are, nobody's *that* cool!

WHAT THE HELL IS WRONG WITH YOU!?

CHAPTER NUMERO DIECISIETE: A GUTSY WAY TO DINE AND DASH?

This is a scam that has been going around for years. I should know, I've seen it everywhere I've worked. It's also a peeve of mine when weak managers let people get away with it. This scam is when someone comes into a restaurant, orders a lavish meal, eats the entire thing, and then complains about how terrible it *WAS*.

I can't speak for everyone out there, but if I really don't like the food that I'm eating, I don't eat it. Besides, I've always eaten with the 'that which does not kill me, makes me stronger' philosophy.

I'm not even one to complain about food when I'm at a restaurant. The only times I will send back food is if it's disgusting to the point of inedibility or has a piece of some employee's anatomy on it. Otherwise, I cope, Even if it's not exactly what I ordered. It's food; I don't want to see food get thrown away (it's that whole world hunger thing).

Now, the scam fits into the category of customer satisfaction, so it's a hard decision for a manager to make. When I was a manager, I didn't find it too hard.

I was working in the training store for Jaybeez family restaurants. I was working a weekday lunch shift. Every weekday, we would get a rush by the surrounding businesses, especially the Wal-Mart that was located right behind us in the same parking lot.

Again, this was the training store; we had the best servers, the quickest cooks, and the best and freshest food in the district. It was all pretty easy. I still had a lot of work to do as the manager like taking care of voids, maintaining the salad bar, throwing potatoes in the oven every hour, help run food, seat people at the

WHAT THE HELL IS WRONG WITH YOU!?

front door, and help the cashiers with the register (all pretty easy, right?).

"Freddy? Table four wants to talk to you. There's a lady there who's not happy with her food." One of the best waitresses (in the world) Sally Fitzgibbons, said to me.

I proceeded to the table that was visible from where I stood behind the cash register. As I walked up, I saw a heavy set woman, dressed in all black, with a couple of Wal-Mart people on the other side of the booth. The Wal-Mart people's backs were turned to me, but it looked as if they were both eating. The woman in black was grazing on her food like she was in the military; fast and furiously. She resembled a pig just let loose on a full trough of food. Now, that wasn't a 'fat joke', it was a true analogy. She was eating like it was some kind of contest you would find in a sick and twisted carnival.

She finished three quarters of her plate *while* I walked the thirty feet from the register to the table. When I got there, I noticed that she was eating breakfast items. I figured this as a good thing because in restaurants, breakfasts only take about three minutes to make.

"Is everything okay here?" I asked in confusion because all three people were polishing off their plates like they were eating in San Quentin. I'm thinking, okay, what's wrong? You all have food, you all have drinks, and you don't seem to have too much of a problem packing it away.

"No," the large woman said to me as she continued to stuff food in her mouth, "this is the worst (swallow) food I've ever (stuff) had (chew). I come here (swallow) all the (stuff) time and have (chew) never had a (swallow) problem until (stuff) now!" It was on of the most amazing things I've ever seen. Through the rudeness of talking to me with a mouthful of food, it was like some new kind of ventriloquisms. It was amazing how bits of eggs and bacon didn't leap from her mouth onto the table.

WHAT THE HELL IS WRONG WITH YOU!?

"Uh, did you want me to make you a new breakfast?" I asked while trying not to laugh.

"Are you kidding? I'm on my lunch break and only have an hour! I don't have the time." She stated while trying not to choke.

"It's really no problem, I could go back there myself and have it made in less than two minutes." Can you tell that I was the 19-year-old 'invincible-kid-manager' that was still nice?

"No, (chew) just forget about (swallow) it now, (stuff) you can (gulp) take this away now," she replied as she handed me an empty plate. The only other two things left she could have done at this point was to lick the plate clean and then start chewing on the porcelain. I let out a little 'okay' and took the plate away, threw it in a bustub, and went back up to the cash register. In my incredulity, I watched as she sat and bullshit with her Wal-Mart friends for **another twenty minutes!** I could then tell that she was in a *really big hurry*.

I think the best part was when she went up to the register to pay.

"Hi there, I think I know how everything was," I said as I loaded her ticket into the computer. Without a word, she handed me her credit card.

"That will be just a second, our credit card machine is kind of slow," I said in a comforting tone. She took the credit card slip, signed it, and emphatically slid it back over the counter to me.

Right after she signed the slip, her floppy jowls opened up and she angrily barked at me, "You know, if you knew how to do your job, you wouldn't have charged me for my food!"

"But ma'am, you ate everything on your plate...as you complained. I can't rationalize having the restaurant pay for things that you had already consumed," I replied.

"Well, I was hungry!" She said getting a little uptight.

What The Hell Is Wrong With You!?

"Why didn't you let me make you new food, I saw that you *did actually have the time*," I said, still in a professional manner.

At that, she decided to skip any remaining pleasantries and shoot right for the throat. I guess just to see if I would back down and void her credit card slip.

"Who's your manager!?" She yelled in the waiting area. So, of course, I gave her the name and phone number of my District Manager right away.

"Feel free to give him a call and let him know the whole story. I'll even note our problem ('challenge' for you resort workers) in the manager's log so we can reference it when he comes to me. Have a nice day, come again!"

Without a word, she spun around like a humungous hooked bowling ball and waddled out the door. We never heard from her again. I honestly hope she didn't choke to death on some food. Talking and eating at the same time is dangerous; especially when no one could perform the Heimlich maneuver on her. Ever try getting your arms around a Winnebago? Exactly.

Moral of the story: Always be cautious when calling someone's bluff, they might not be bluffing and have a bigger hand.

What The Hell Is Wrong With You!?

Chapter Numero Dieciocho: One Irrelevant Point That Needs Addressing

I was second guessing even putting this in because it has nothing to do with a bar or restaurant, just stupid people. I put it in because some of my friends at the airport agreed that it belongs.

This actually happens to me (and other restaurant employees in the airport) walking through the airport on my way to the bar. In many airports these days, there are moving walkways between the concourses. There is one thing I need to denote about these walkways.

I try to remind myself of this fact everyday. The moving walkways are for conserving energy and not necessarily to save time. You can, however, save time if you walk full stride when no one is in the way. This is where the problem comes from. Normally, I'm a quick walker. Working in restaurants will do this to a person. I also sometimes have a problem getting into the concourse on time everyday due to one thing or another. For instance, I won't be able to find a parking space or I'll miss the shuttle-bus, what have you.

Apparently, I'm not the only person at the airport with this gripe. There are two things that get on our nerves, and probably the nerves of *regular* people as well. There are signs above the walkways that read, STAND ON THE RIGHT/WALK ON THE LEFT. There is also a recording that sounds about every fifteen to twenty seconds that says, "While using the moving walkway, please stand to the right so that others can pass safely on the left."

McCarren International Airport in Las Vegas, for instance, it's even printed on the walkway itself. One side says 'WALK' and the other, 'STAND'.

WHAT THE HELL IS WRONG WITH YOU!?

It's just like driving a car, but we all know how many dolts can't figure out the four-word phrase, 'SLOWER TRAFFIC KEEP RIGHT'. There will always be that moron in the fast lane of the highway doing 50 miles an hour.

Back to the airport, people will stand, three or four at a time, smack dab in the middle of the walkway. You would think that the backup of twenty or so people behind them would give them a clue to move, but it rarely does. They are either just inconsiderate bastards or they're too busy looking out the window at the shiny airplanes.

* * *

The other thing that you should never do is to take those rental luggage carts onto the walkway. What's more, not moving the cart down the walkway, but just have it stopped like a stalled car on a narrow bridge. The cart takes up the entire walkway, don't be rude!

This is what I have done in a similar situation. I was in Las Vegas and wanted to use the moving walkway. I used them not because I was in a hurry, but because I wanted to just stand. I had one of those carts with me. As I entered the walkway, I pushed the cart onto the outside of the railing and towed it along. I stayed on the 'STAND' side so the cart was in no one's way. Airline employees would applaud and exclaim "Hey, good idea!" to me because they feel the same pain, and everything was right in the world.

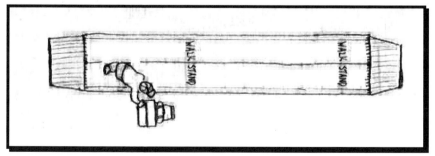

What The Hell Is Wrong With You!?

Chapter Diecinueve: Vodka, By Definition, Is An Odorless, Tasteless, Distilled Grain Liquor

To go along with the person that said that he couldn't taste the alcohol in his frou-frou drinks comes another edition to this particular breed of customer.

First off, the more you spend on vodka, the less you will 'feel' the alcohol. This truth is, unless it's flavored vodka, vodka doesn't have much of a distinction. Working in a bar where Smirnoff is our well, it's hard to please some people.

I will agree that normal well vodkas that you would find in a bar will have somewhat of a taste…it's usually yuck. Here's a good realization on well vodka at normal bars. Pick up a bottle from the well next time you get a chance and find out where it's from. You may be surprised. Most of the vodkas that I have worked with are from Kentucky. Not imported by a company in Kentucky…from Kentucky. There's another reason for me to stay out of Kentucky.

For a person that orders a Skyy vodka screwdriver, all they will taste is the orange juice. This is what makes Skyy one of my favorite vodkas. If you ever get a chance give it a try, it's good stuff.

If you really think that vodka has an alcohol taste that you desire, other than a burn, order it on the rocks. As a matter of fact, you can do this with any drink. If you can't taste the alcohol, ask for either a 'splash' of mixer, or just order your favorite liquor on the rocks. Or just do shots. Either way, you will taste the alcohol then! If at this point you still can't taste the alcohol, switch up to Everclear. You won't have a problem then. If that <u>still</u> doesn't do it for you, you may have to move to the really hard stuff, rubbing alcohol, gasoline, and turpentine. Good stuff for the first night or so, but then you die. Hey, I guess it would beat the hangover, right?

(Legal Disclaimer: The sentence about 'the really hard stuff' is used as a joke. Please do not try to consume alcohols of a burning or cleaning nature. Using these products for reasons different from their original purpose could be harmful to your health or fatal in some cases. Not to mention, with some products, would be in violation of certain federal laws. It sickens me that I have to put this in.)

What The Hell Is Wrong With You!?

Chapter Numero Veinte: Why Did You Even Ask For A Refill!?

This pet peeve of mine ranks way up there on the list and I know anyone who works in restaurants know exactly what I'm talking about. Just in case you don't know, I've included a little diagram to help you along.

When I am really busy, I will usually wind up having one or two people do this. I honestly think it's just to waste my time. As I run by this person at one of my tables or at the bar that has already finished eating and paid, they will ask me for a refill on his or her soda. I tell him or her 'okay' and that I will get it in just a minute. I come right back with hands full of food and drinks for other people (following my mental list), and the same person will ask again for a drink refill. I respond with a generic 'just a minute' phrase. On my way back from the table or area of the bar that I just dropped off all the food, this person will ask again (This time I never even left his field of vision!). Less than one minute has passed since this person asked the first time, showing obvious refill impertinence. Out of frustration, I drop what I'm doing to get this person their soda refill so they will stop bugging the ever-loving shit out of me. I drop this person's glass off. When I turn around just a few seconds later, they're gone. What they leave behind them astonishes me. This person will take **one more sip** out of their soda and split.

WHAT THE HELL IS WRONG WITH YOU!?

What's up with that!? I have never in my life needed just one more sip of soda. It's usually hard for me to suck down whatever soda I have left when I go out. What a waste! Sure, I know that a glass of soda costs a restaurant five to eight cents, but it all adds up. And it's still a waste of my precious time! Chew on an ice cube! Damn.

WHAT THE HELL IS WRONG WITH YOU!?

CHAPTER NUMERO VEINTIUNO: SO YOU THINK YOU KNOW YOUR TEQUILAS AND MARGARITAS, EH?

We've already established the importance of not ordering the best tequila in the house unless you are sure of yourself. I just need to point this out for everyone in the rest of the world that really doesn't know their tequilas – and do a bad job pretending.

If you call out tequilas by their names, you should know a little about it. At least you should know what a Cuervo product is. I guess it bugs me because it happens so often where I work now. When you walk up to the bar in any bar in an airport in America run by 'PMS toast', you will see that there are three or four bottles of each and every liquor served at that particular bar. It's policy to have these bottles there for promotional purposes and to help out the customer. Jose Cuervo products are the only tequilas we serve in our bar. That would exclude all tequilas NOT made by Jose Cuervo.

This is like the beer tap situation, except the customer has to focus on something up to six feet away as opposed to eight inches away from their face.

"Do you have Herradura?" customers have asked on numerous occasions.

"No, all we have is Cuervo products." I say back to them as I point to my shirt that says so, or display the wall behind me with my hand showing the tequilas we do have.

"Oh, do you have Patron?"

"No, but we do have Centenario, which is Cuervo's equivalent."

"Oh, well, do you have Tres (Generaciones)?"

"No, all we have is Cuervo products."

"Okay, Don Julio?"

"No, Cuervo."

WHAT THE HELL IS WRONG WITH YOU!?

"How about Cabo Wabo?"

"No, Cuervo."

"Do you have…"

"No. How about a nice shot of 1800?"

Sometimes we have to draw a little picture for these people, it's truly amazing.

I know that this one is a little unfair, because someone could like Patron and not know that it is it's own company and not made by Cuervo. But if you ask for a product by name, amongst others that I work with that feel the same as I, you should know.

* * *

This is something that I never thought I would have to bring up. My mind sees it as common knowledge. However, due to recent events, I find that I'm required to add this in.

First of all, when you make a margarita, you're pretty much mixing tequila, triple sec (very little alcohol, orange flavor, and sugar) and sweet and sour mix (mostly sugar). If you ask for a margarita to taste a majority of tequila, a margarita probably isn't what you really want. Remember back in the day, when Mary Poppins said, "A spoon-full of sugar helps the medicine go down"? Yeah, same shit.

Secondly, when you take that same margarita and stick it in a blender, it becomes watered down! Let me explain a couple things about the physical properties involved living in this dimension. Liquid aids in the melting of frozen items. Miniscule shreds of ice, like the ones found in a frozen margarita, will melt faster than large chunks of ice. When you put a portion of your frozen margarita in your mouth, now you add heat to the equation. As we all know especially in Arizona, heat melts…everything! All of the 'little ice cubes' in a frozen margarita further melt down as you swish the concoction around in your mouth. Movement, like stirring your straw in your margarita also furthers the melting process. All of these, in turn, water down your margarita.

What The Hell Is Wrong With You!?

Just in case there are still a few reading this that are lost – *ice is water*. I'm not kidding, it is! It's just really hard and cold.

Now that I've briefly explained some of the attributes of thermodynamics and the sciences of the material world, I'll tell you the story behind my need for the explanation.

I was bartending in a Mexican restaurant where, following the theme, margaritas were a pretty big deal. We pre-made our house margaritas and kept them in a large machine. These margaritas were just as strong as any other margarita that I would make by hand. One of my customers was your stereotypical wannabe California surfer-type. He was sporting the messy bleached hair look, expensive watch, Bermuda shorts, and sandals that looked like they were kept in the box at night. Him and his buddy ordered a couple frozen margaritas. I asked them if they wanted a pitcher so it would be cheaper for them and easier for me. Everyone wins. They agreed so I retrieved their drink order. When I returned back to the table, the idiot spoke.

"Is there any tequila in here at all? Am I just missing it? Is it all on the bottom of the pitcher?" He asked me the barrage of non-essential questions as he stirred up his margarita with his straw.

Choosing to answer the first and third question, I returned with, "Our margaritas are pre-made in the margarita machine behind the bar."

"Oh, well I just spent a month in Mexico and I can't taste any alcohol here." He stupidly remarked as he pointed to his glass. All the things I could have said here:

- Mexico doesn't have to many laws mandating how much alcohol can legally be served to one person.
- Tequila is dirt cheap in Mexico, where here we have 'pour cost'.
- Frozen margaritas could be considered frou-frou drinks.
- You're an idiot.

182

What The Hell Is Wrong With You!?

Instead of those four, I chose to take the marketing approach.

"Well, would you like a shot of tequila on the side to add to it?" I asked.

"Would that be on the house then?"

What, in trade for your brilliance? Why don't I just bring you the bottle?

"No, I'm afraid I can't do that." I said.

"Well, it's okay then, it's fine." He said giving up his argument. I took their food order and turned it into the kitchen. On the way back from the kitchen to the bar, I figured I would see what he had to say when I hit him with the explicit logic stated before.

"You know guys, if you want, I can get you a new pitcher of margarita on the rocks, you'll be able to taste the alcohol more if it's not frozen." I stated.

"So there's more alcohol in the drink when you make it on the rocks?" He knew about the machine, right?

"No, no…when you blend a drink with ice, it becomes watered-down because the ice melts quicker." I said as he looked at me like he was lost in an extravagant amusement park.

"Do, do you know what I mean? You melt the ice in your mouth as you drink the margarita. That won't happen when it's on the rocks, unless you normally chew your margaritas."

"No entiendo, no entiendo!" He said in a very bad 'spanglish' accent as he laughed to his buddy. 'No entiendo' means 'I don't understand' in Spanish. I bet he said that all the time when he was in Mexico.

What The Hell Is Wrong With You!?

Another thing about tequilas that I want to add in for you is about 'blue margaritas'. A blue margarita is any kind of lime-flavored margarita that you want with an addition of a liquor called Blue Curaco – it's blue and it's orange flavored. *Blue Agave* on the other hand is a cactus. These plants are what make tequila possible.

I have had many people come up to the bar and ask for a 'blue agave margarita'. These people are just asking for a regular margarita! I know that this is more of an education thing and not many people, including restaurant employees, know about the genre *agave*. This doesn't really make me too angry, it's just annoying. Food for thought.

What The Hell Is Wrong With You!?

Chapter Numero Veintidos: If You Order It ~ It Will Come...Both Times!

There are people in this world that have no comprehension on how a restaurant works. This includes the people that get their own drinks out of the service well, people that walk up to the pass through window in a full service restaurant and ask the cooks for food, and my favorite, the person that orders twice. Let me explain:

Every once in a while, Mr. Idiot will come in and sit down at a table, be greeted right away, and will have his order taken. The server will ring in the order. In case you don't know this, even if it's completely dead, it may still take one or even up to two minutes for Mr. Idiot to receive his drink. When it's busy, it could be up to three or four minutes. I talked about that whole 'consolidation' thing before. No server will bring out one drink at a time to a station; they will bring out many drinks at one time.

Now then, Mr. Idiot has already ordered. He will figure that two minutes is just too damn long to wait. He will go up to the bar and order the same drink again.

Not only is this incredibly uncouth, but it's wrong for so many reasons. Thirty seconds later when the server returns to see that the same kind of drink that the server is delivering, is sitting in front of his fat face. This is where all the problems present themselves. First of all, the server will think that they have another server's drink and return it to the bartender, wasting valuable time and energy. Secondly, it's a waste of product, which could be misconstrued as alcohol abuse (Ha ha.). Third, Mr. Idiot just took extra time away from the bartender who had to make the same drink for the same person...**twice!**

When the server realizes that they're holding an extra drink that goes nowhere, the server gets upset. This is a scenario taken from my experience starting at that point.

What The Hell Is Wrong With You!?

"So. You went to the bar, I see." I said.

"Yep, had to, you just took too long." Mr. Idiot said without any remorse. This made me angrier because it wasted a lot of my time and energy and this fucking moron doesn't even care enough to apologize for his fuck up.

"You know you only waited about a minute and a half for me to come back."

"Well, hey, I was thirsty. I couldn't wait." Mr. Idiot responded.

"Well, hey," I said as I sat the second drink down on his table, "you ordered this one as well, so you have to pay for it."

"Bullshit I do, I already have my drink."

"Otherwise, I have to pay for it and it's just going to be wasted. That will be $5.15." I said.

Now, at this point, Mr. Idiot will do one of two things. I'll let you guess which road this particular 'Mr. Idiot' took. Either they will reluctantly pay for the second drink understanding that they did order it twice, but they won't tip you anything if they can help it. Or they will demand to talk to the manager. Following the formula from chapter six, the two minutes that he actually waited has now turned to nine. When Mr. Idiot talks to the manager, the manager will apologize and take the other drink away and throw it in the sink.

Let's go back to my situation, which path do you think Mr. Idiot followed? You probably guessed right. He chose path number two. Even though I didn't really have to pay for the other drink, it still pissed me off that he didn't. Granted, I bluffed at the airport, but at a lot of bars I've worked at before, I would have had to pay. Mr. Idiot consequently had to go to the bar and didn't get served from me for the rest of his stay. I'm too slow.

Moral of the story for all you 'Mr. Idiot's' out there: no matter where you are in the world or what you are ordering, if you order something twice from two different people, it will equal two

WHAT THE HELL IS WRONG WITH YOU!?

separate transactions. Think of it this way, walk into a car dealership and order a car, pick your colors and options, and then find another salesperson and do the same thing again. Come delivery day, you might have two cars there. Duh.

What The Hell Is Wrong With You!?

Chapter Numero Veintitres: What Is Your Problem With The Furniture? I Mean Really

People will always go into a restaurant and move the tables and chairs around to accommodate their needs. More than half of the time, they will either screw up the server's sections, put tables in places that servers need to walk, or they will make it damn near impossible to reach far enough to set shit down. Wait a minute, who am I kidding? I mean *all* the time. I don't think I have ever had customers move tables in a way that doesn't affect one or more of the things listed above. Usually, I try to catch them as soon as they slide a chair away from the table to assist them. This works pretty well and isn't even what really pisses me off...it's the chairs.

Nobody seems to use their brain when it comes to these two things. I've illustrated them for better comprehension. Both of these things happen at the bar and at the tables.

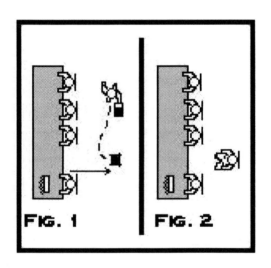

What The Hell Is Wrong With You!?

Figure one. As you can see, the customer that was in seat number two has just left. When he leaves, he will push his chair or barstool backwards into the walkway behind him *and just leave it there!* I don't know how the majority of people in this world were brought up, but 'push in you chair' was every one of my grade school teacher's favorite sayings. What I really like to see is when four or five people do it all at once so the walkways are littered with chairs. And then they all have to simultaneously struggle in their own disarray! I finally get to laugh! Yes!

* * *

Figure two follows the same physical properties as figure one, except for one thing. The guest doesn't remove his fat ass from the chair. Many times people have put their chairs or barstools right out in the middle of nothing. It's literally beyond me how these people can do this without, at the least, feeling awkward.

For me, thanks to Murphy's Law, when I need to walk through that particular walkway, I will be holding seven drinks or maybe four plates in one hand and a couple pizzas on my other arm. What puts me on Prozac is when I have to ask them to move.

"Excuse me, please don't sit in a walkway." I say this in a loud, stressed tone. These idiots will either do, again, one of two things. Number one, they will jump out of their chairs, apologize, and immediately move out of the way. This is obviously the right thing to do. This happens on rare occasions. The sad part is when they sit back down where they were in the middle of the walkway. I guess they figure that I'd only be by once. Even though is shows that they were in the wrong and were willing to comply, it also shows their blatant disrespect for other humans that *can actually think.*

Number two. They slowly look over to me holding all of my items, notice that I've got a full load and angrily glare at me. That's right, glare at me like I just asked them to sacrifice their

WHAT THE HELL IS WRONG WITH YOU!?

first born to the god of small trees. These idiots will grudgingly move like his sciatica nerve just burst. Just to put the frosting on the damn cake, they too will sit back down in the same place they were before. Then to put lit candles on that same cake, they will still get just as disturbed when I or another server has to walk by and ask him to move again, and again, and again. If you are one of these people, just don't go out anymore! You're grounded…go to your room!

What The Hell Is Wrong With You!?

Chapter Numero Veinticuatro: I'm Telling You That You're An Idiot! Can You Tell Me When I Make A Mistake?

Like I said in the beginning, nobody is perfect. This definitely includes me. There are times when I will screw something up. It could be because I'm really busy and flustered, or it could be because it's so dead in the bar that I'm fighting just to stay awake. It happens to everyone so I'm not too ashamed to talk about it.

When a customer corrects me, I apologize and fix what I did wrong. If I'm not in the wrong, I will tactfully say something to correct them. If someone sees me prepare or make the wrong item, I thank him or her for correcting me. I don't like to waste. Granted, this doesn't happen all to often, usually only when I'm really tired and/or hung over. When it's slow and someone knows I'm making his or her drink wrong and doesn't correct me, then I have a problem. Let me give you and example:

A customer walks up to the bar and orders a beer. I pull the wrong tap handle by accident. It happens, shows that I too, am human. I could do this because I'm checking on someone else down the bar or look at the server printer for drink orders, what have you. When I looking back over, I forgot which domestic beer the guy had ordered. Here's the clincher. I will set down the wrong beer to the person and they will say something like, "That don't look like Bud."

Okay, you got me; you even got to be a little cocky – good for you! Now why the hell didn't you tell me while I poured it? It becomes personal to me at that point. See, here's the thing. Beer and me go way back and I've grown a kinship with the merciful/merciless amber liquid. I don't like to waste it. Even though I do not share that kinship with the lesser genre, *brew domestica*, it still shouldn't be wasted. So do the beer kingdom a

WHAT THE HELL IS WRONG WITH YOU!?

favor, don't let this happen to you. Remember – waste not, want not!

What The Hell Is Wrong With You!?

Chapter Numero Veinticinco: I Think You Need The Library, Not The Airport

Here's another little anecdote from Becca at the airport. I really didn't believe her at first, but then I thought, 'we're at the airport, and we're surrounded by idiots.'

Two ladies came into the bar because their flight to Atlanta was delayed. They were talking about the people in Atlanta they were planning to meet for their rides. They realized that they didn't have a phone number to contact them. These women, God bless them, asked their server in an airport bar, in Phoenix, Arizona if they could see an Atlanta phone book.

I find this incredibly strange because of the circumstances. It's all about location kids. Actually, I would find it even stranger if we did have a phone book from another city. Hell, we don't even have a phone book for Phoenix in the bar. I can't talk about this anymore; it's hurting my head.

What The Hell Is Wrong With You!?

Chapter Numero Veintiseis: If You Are Hungry, Eat The Damn Food!

This story could have fit into the time management chapter, but it needed special attention. When people do this to me, it raises my anger level so high it makes my blood boil.

A customer will walk in and sit down in the restaurant to order food. Regardless if they look like they are in a hurry, I treat them like anyone else. This customer will order a drink and some food. The actual story that I'm thinking about happened only three months ago at the airport. Keep in mind that this scenario happens all of the time.

He was a businessman dressed in adequate attire. He maintained a cellular conversation through the duration of his stay. He never took off his trench coat. It was a moderately busy day and his food took about fifteen minutes. These were actual minutes, not *airport time* (see chapter six) or anything. I brought it out to his table. As I walked up, I noticed that he was gathering up his belongings with his free hand. The other hand was still holding the cell phone to his head. He looks up and sees me holding his food.

"Oh, just cancel my order! It took to long, I have to go." He told me bypassing his cell phone. (That's…why…too…angry…Burger King!!)

Like I've mentioned before, voids at the airport are a huge pain in the ass. I tired to help myself not have a void and help the customer at the same time.

"I could wrap it up to go for you in thirty seconds, you can eat it on the plane." I tried to barter.

"No, I don't have the time. I guess I'll just have to starve!"

I don't care where you are, thirty seconds isn't going to make a rat's ass difference in anything; unless you are in a race of some kind – but not at the airport. I've worked in the airport for

WHAT THE HELL IS WRONG WITH YOU!?

almost a year now and have traveled on airplanes many, many times in my life. I have never, ever even heard of someone missing a plane by thirty seconds!

So he asked me how much he owed for the drink. I told him and he handed me a credit card. First thing I thought was it would take, in normal circumstances, more than thirty seconds to run your credit card. Duh.

I was at a new point in my anger's history. His obvious lack of logic had made me so upset that I didn't tell him the process I will need to go through. I would have to cash out his old check, start a new one, and run his credit card on the new one. This process would take about three times longer than for him to just take the food with him. It's right fucking here! Of course, I took my time to get his check to him. The best part of the story: did he miss his flight? No. I made sure that he made it, just so I could tell you for the end of this story

What The Hell Is Wrong With You!?

Chapter Veintisiete: Did You Want To Eat From That Ashtray?

Ironically, this person wasn't the 'Mr. Fourstar' mentioned before, but had the same M.O.

This customer walked up to the bar in the airport and sat down. Lying in front of him were two ashtrays. Being one of the only designated smoking areas in the airport, it's hard to keep an ashtray clean for more than a minute and a half. One of the ashtrays was empty, but dirty on the bottom. The other one had two butts sitting in it.

"Excuse me, can I get an ashtray?" He says to me in a snobbish tone. When I looked over, I noticed that both ashtrays were in arm's reach of the man. He wouldn't even have to stretch. Seeing that he was oblivious to his surroundings and obviously not a master in the science of reasoning, I stopped what I was doing and slowly slid the ashtray without the cigarette butts over to him. Maybe it was twelve inches away.

"Ugh," he snorts and laughs at the same time, "Can I get a *clean* one?" His tone was beyond the threshold of normal. His mannerisms showed that maybe he belonged in Buckingham Palace, however his attitude belonged in Chuck E Cheese.

I took the other ashtray with the butts in it, emptied it out, wiped out the bottom with a cocktail napkin and slid that one over too him.

"Puishh..." As he expelled that familiar 'bus stopping noise' I've described before, he smoked his thin cigarette in his delicate little fingers. He never looked back at me, nor the television, or anything else. He just stared at the ceiling in his tribulation for my uncouth actions. Hey, shit for brains, your smoking a cigarette! It's not the cleanest habit in the world. What do you think your lungs look like? I guarantee that they are not necessarily limpid. I'm sure mine are in the shape of a Camel by now!

You know, to this day, I don't even know if he wanted a drink or not. I was too disgusted to ask.

What The Hell Is Wrong With You!?

Chapter Veintiocho: Mind Your P's (Cigarettes) and Q's (Gum)

I apologize for this small occurrence of redundancy, but I have to point out a couple of things again because they really, really piss me off.

Nothing shows class like using a glass as an ashtray. I cannot stress enough how terrible this is! Don't be an inconsiderate imbecile! It's really gross. You know that I smoke so you know that my opinion is unbiased. Please.

* * *

The other thing I need to hit again is the bad habits with gum. Knock off sticking used gum under chairs and tables! Would you do that at home? I don't like touching the filth that was in your mouth God knows how long ago. Show a little respect, please.

* * *

There is one other thing that I need to address in this chapter. I had actually forgotten about it until it happened (again) at the bar tonight. Thank God in heaven that I remembered this because it is of utmost importance to the health and safety of us all. Do not ever leave your disgusting, putrid, bloody, infectious, used <u>bandages</u> (!) on the bar or a table for your server to clean up. Nobody wants to touch your filthy shit! We don't know where you've been. Furthermore, we don't want to know. Really, a garbage receptacle can't possible be that hard to find. Please, I implore you, don't leave self-adhesive biohazards lying around where food and drinks are served. It's sick!

For those of you out there that think no one could possibly do this, be lucky that you have never had to experience it before. Takes a real idiot to pull off stupid shit like that, I mean it. Gross!

WHAT THE HELL IS WRONG WITH YOU!?

CHAPTER VEINTINUEVE: A FEW CLASSIC QUOTES OR PERFORMANCES THAT NEED ADDRESSING

Irony at it's finest

This was a question by a couple of customers at the airport. Two older ladies came into the bar to light up a couple cigarettes. They both walked into Becca's station. One of the ladies took a puff or two of her cigarette and then began to look around for something. Like the illustration shows back on page 50, our bar at the airport has a small patio section. At the airport, due to the law, smoking in the concourse is strictly prohibited and marked as such. The one lady walked over to Becca and asked one of the most ass backwards question I've ever heard:

"Can we smoke on the patio? I can't smoke in here, it smells too much like food."

I'm not kidding. I guess we could have asked the rest of the people in the bar to *put out their burritos*.

Levels of drunkenness

Everyone should know when to say when. 'Should' being the operative word. Not many people really know when to quit. For those that do, they are usually teased and coaxed into drinking more anyway.

For everyone else it's pretty much the same. When they think it's time to say when, they can't remember how to say when, and why would they say when then anyhow? Did I loose you? I lost myself. Drink a few more beers and read it again, it'll make perfect sense.

Everyone should follow my lead on this one. I think it's one of the best ideas I've had and it would actually constitute something being learned from this book.   I have done this throughout the later half of my drinking career (yes, it's a career). I made a list of things that I do as I progress into the six different levels of inebriation.   I call it my 'levels of drunkenness'.   I then gave this list to a few of my friends to keep an eye on me on those certain nights where it was a mission to have three sheets to the wind.   Here's a personalized list of my levels of drunkenness that still hold true to this day:

1. Flipping my R's in words like 'tree' and 'three' (I can thank my Spanish teacher for that one)
2. Sudden and unexpected *NEED* to play any game of any kind
3. Singing out loud, with or without music playing
4. Vacant stares into space
5. Dancing…very poorly
6. Paralysis

Once again, every friend should have a list like this.   That friend shouldn't let anyone reach level six.   That is unless the observer is already at level six. Then just dial 911.

The best hangover line I've ever heard

Being a conditioned drinker, I've used many different excuses for being hungover.   I've blamed my scatterbrained ways and tardiness on everything starting from car problems all the way to alien abduction.   Granted, luckily for me it hasn't recently been a daily activity, but more often than anyone would like.   I usually have to break down and tell the truth why I'm into work hungover. Honesty is the best policy, especially if you come into work in the morning to the same damn bar you were drinking at the night

WHAT THE HELL IS WRONG WITH YOU!?

before. It's a little harder to deceive your manager that was there the night before as well.

One of my friends, Mike, works at a car dealership. He holds the same philosophy of honesty. Mike made it into work after a long Friday night.

"Mike, you're late. And you smell like beer!" Mike's boss told him.

"Yeah, I feel like beer." Mike replied.

Just goes to show you, you are what you eat, or drink. Thanks Mike!

Cops can have a sense of humor too

My friend Ruby that I worked with before told me this story at the epoch of her understanding of the joke.

Four of Tempe's police officers came into the restaurant for lunch. These four in particular have lunch at this place quite often. Ruby went to the table to deliver their food:

"Here you go guys," Ruby said as she set their food down, "And I brought you guys some extra napkins because I know that you usually leave a mess."

"Are you calling us pigs?" One of the officers replied.

Ruby didn't get it at first, but when she did, she was quick to tell me about the situation. The next time the cop came in; he said that he wanted the royalties to his joke. Well, sorry brother. I hope you don't pull me over!

You weren't there man!

This is a real simple quick laugh for you. Even the vet's can laugh at this one. I had this table of four that looked like a family. A husband, wife, daughter, and looked liked a grandma. They all drank soda except for dad; he drank beer. They all seemed pretty normal. No one did anything obscure until I asked them if they wanted dessert.

"Did any of you guys save any room for dessert?" I asked.

"No, are you kidding?" The mom replied.

"Oh, no (laughing) I ate too much already!" Grandma said.

"I don't have room." The daughter said.

"When I was in Nam, I'd never eat dessert!" Dad replied.

WHAT!? Where the hell did that come from? I hope he didn't have some kind of flashback of being held hostage by a Ding-Dong and a Twinkie speaking in foreign tongues. Keep it down; you're scaring the kid. More so, you're scaring me.

WHAT THE HELL IS WRONG WITH YOU!?

CHAPTER NUMERO TREINTA: MANAGERIAL ABUSE

All of my managers in the past ten years have been significant to me. Well, in one-way or another.

Bill Phares got me to start smoking cigarettes (yeah!). He didn't twist my arm or anything, but he was my influence. He also helped me learn Spanish about ten years ago. He often brandished his .44 magnum handgun (like the one in *Robocop*) from his brief case and yell 'BAM' at the top of his voice leaving us to defecate ourselves.

Gordon seemed to erringly follow a similar path as I did. We wound up working together at Jaybeez Restaurants, Copper's Sports Bar, and a small deli that was in the Scottsdale Airpark. Showing that this is, in fact, a small world after all.

Jan Herrera, who is my manager at the airport, always threatened everyone that she would 'shove her ten-and-a-half all up in someone's ass'. I especially put this in here because if I didn't, she said that she would shove her ten-and-a-half all up in my ass. She also offered oodles of solace on my Sunday morning shifts; those were my 'hangover shifts'. She would also bet everyone working on which time I would come in for my shift, be it right on time, at 4:00, or 4:03, 4:05, etc. She'd usually win. That is until one of my friends got smart and the secret got out that he would call my cell phone to make sure I arrived at a certain time. Then we would have split the money. Oh well.

But by far one of the most influential managers I've ever had has to be Jake Guzman. He also became one of my close friends. We've been through the thick and thin together. However, I think when I worked at McDuffy's, he fired me something like eight times. Wrote me up (written disciplinary action) about thirty or forty times. This one time that he fired me, he even had security escort me off the premises after signing my termination paperwork. Then, no more than two minutes later, he would come back outside and yell at me for not being in my station. It was a lot of fun working with that dude.

I could go on forever listing people that have made a difference to me. Again, you know who you are and feel free to scribble your name in the margin. Thank you all.

What The Hell Is Wrong With You!?

Chapter Numero Treintiuno ~ International Restaurant Signs

This is a quick little chapter used to cover the international restaurant signs. These signs are known by most; but I feel that there are enough people in this world that just don't know them well enough. This guide is for them.

For those of you who are unsure of these signs, they are hand signals used to communicate to your bartender or server without the use of words. I will list them in order of the most used first:

o Check – There are a few ways to perform this sign. First, and most common, with your right hand, pantomime holding a pen and scribble in the air. Second, with your finger or the pantomimed pen, make a giant check mark in front of you. Third, pretend to write something down on your opposing hand. Sometimes you can just mouth the word 'check' – usually this is added to all three actions above.

o Round – Make a circular motion with your hand and extended pointer finger either pointing directly down at the table, or strait up in the air.

o Refill or Another – Point directly down at an item or a soda glass.

o Clean this table or Oops, I spilled – With an open palm, take your right hand and in a circular motion, hover your hand over the table like Mr. Miyagi's 'wax the car' move in *The Karate Kid*.

o Okay, Cool, or Correct – make a fist and extend your thumb upwards, pretty normal

WHAT THE HELL IS WRONG WITH YOU!?

○ Denote quantity – In the United states, extend the amount of fingers of the hand to show how many of the items in question you desire. Little tidbit of useless trivia for you: I learned in Mexico, you have to start that count with your thumb being number one. If you hold up your pointer and middle finger to mean two, you might receive three because they might count your thumb as one.

○ Help, I'm choking – While not being able to breath, hold your right hand over your throat and gasp for air.

* * *

Here is a situation to justify the listing of these signs. I was working a busy game-day at McDuffy's Sports Bar in Tempe. The entire restaurant was at capacity. As I scanned my tables from the computer station for refills or dirty plates, one of my tables (table 112) tried to communicate with me.

He took his hand and connected his thumb to the ends of his fingers as if he was wearing a sock-puppet. He then made like a nodding motion with his hand as if he had a piece of yarn and was playing 'keep away' with a kitten.

He kept doing this motion with more and more intensity as I shrugged my shoulders and shook my head to show that I couldn't understand what he was saying. I started making guesses, "Yo-yo? Pecking bird? Marionette? Car keys? What do you want?"

"The check!" he yelled back in frustration.

How was that supposed to mean 'check'? That wasn't in the aforementioned listing anywhere. I guess if he expected us to use some sort of punch card system to tabulate his bill. I don't know.

WHAT THE HELL IS WRONG WITH YOU!?

CHAPTER NUMERO TREINTIDOS: PRACTICAL JOKES ~ OF COURSE YOU REALIZE, THIS MEANS WAR *–Bugs Bunny*

Just so this entire thing I've created doesn't wind up bitter in its entirety I'm going to throw in a few added bonuses.

Practical jokes, if you don't already know, have been and always will be a thick slab in the foundation of restaurant work. It usually becomes more of an elaborate art form than the old 'plastic wrap on the toilet seat and Ex-Lax chocolate cake' trick. Though funny, it always leaves one hell of a mess to clean up. Some of the best ones that I've seen have been monumental. I've actually been entertained by them all with my low entertainment value. I've laughed from one extreme to the next. The simple ones: putting a layer of ketchup in the bottom of a coworker's sealed drink. To the mediocre ones: powdering your nostrils with a powdered donut and walking around like you're about to freak out. To the more elaborate ones: when we took the manager's keys from the back door that he forget, moved his car, and then told him it was stolen. Ahh, good times! But all in fun.

* * *

This chapter is actually a little one-day war I had with a coworker of mine from McDuffy's. It was a true contest of wits and skill; and to the victor, the fruits of knowing who's best.

I need to start by telling you about my friend and opponent, Tommy. He was a bartender that I had been working with for about two years. He was, and probably still is one of the biggest flirts I've ever seen. As soon as a girl would come into the bar and sit down, sure as shit, he'd be the first one there trying to massage them or show them a bar trick. Don't get me wrong; I find nothing wrong with this. I'm the same way. I'm just more selective with women. He takes the whole fruit basket. Just so you know,

WHAT THE HELL IS WRONG WITH YOU!?

Tommy isn't just some schmuck that you would normally run into; he's a much better schmuck than that.

Now then, Tommy and I never did decide who won the battle. So you can all draw your own conclusions.

It all started one night when a couple of girls that were becoming regulars at the bar came in for happy hour. The whole thing started by me cocking off to Tommy, and in a show of territorialism, he sprayed me with the soda gun from behind the bar. He then went back to the girls.

A little while later, I noticed that in one of the girls glasses of water, he constructed a three foot straw out of five regular straws. Clever. The girls got a kick out of it when he would drink through the straws. They giggled and carried on with Tommy, until it was time for my revenge. I waited until Tommy went into the kitchen, my moment to strike. When he was in the back, I took a bottle of Tabasco and filled up about four of the five straws. I told the girls to tell Tommy to take another drink. I walked away for a little while, serviced my tables, and returned right in time. I stood at the far end of the bar when he drank about a third of a bottle of Tabasco, with a little water to spread the fire around. It took him about five or six seconds to taste the Tabasco, but when he did, his flirty little 'hey there!' smile dropped to a scowl as he slowly turned his head to peer down at me laughing.

"Now it's on Freddy, you don't know who you're messing with buddy! Oh, it's on." Tommy said as I continued to jeer. We all know how the saying goes; he who laughs last, laughs best (or loudest, shoot, I'm not sure. I guess *I* don't know, sorry!) The proverbial ball was now in his court.

A little bit later, one of the two girls patted me on the back to congratulate me for what I did and tell me how funny it was. I said thanks and went back to work. Anyone reading this guess what just happened? That's right. I fell for the oldest practical joke known to man. It was the old 'slap the note on the back' trick. Son of a bitch!

Showing an abrupt raise in the game, Tommy elected to bypass the simplicity of the joke. The sign on my back didn't say 'kick me', nor did it say something simple like 'idiot' or 'stooge'; it said, 'I like cock'. I walked around for about 45 minutes oblivious to the sign on my back. I really couldn't figure out what the hell was so damn funny, but everyone was laughing. The customers were laughing, the girls at the bar were laughing, security was laughing, but the most disturbing factor was Tommy was laughing. It didn't even click when one of the drunken customers approached me with a smile and asked if I liked cock. Now I'm running around like a dog chasing his tail trying to find something on me. I checked for blue pool cue chalk on my face, one of those toilet seat protectors hanging out of the back of my pants, or shit in my hair; all to no avail. Finally the manager, Jake Guzman walked up behind me, ripped off the sign and handed it to me in utter disgust. I immediately knew what had happened. Point: Tommy.

I waited for a little while for Tommy to leave the bar again. When he did, I took his car keys that he foolishly left hanging up behind the bar. About an hour or so had past by. Tommy kept egging me on to wait until the end of the night. It was then that I would see the grand finale. For the rest of the night, we were good to each other. The girls had long gone since the beginning, however I knew it wasn't over. With both of us watching our own backs, we waited and wondered what the other one had done or was planning to do. The end of the night approached. I went to the back of the restaurant to get Tommy's keys.

"Hey, Tommy?" I said in a calm voice.

"Yeah Freddy." He replied.

"What's really hard and cold and goes to your car?"

"I don't know Freddy, what?"

WHAT THE HELL IS WRONG WITH YOU!?

"Your keys." I said as I lifted them up. I encased them in a large frozen block of ice. I think he was actually proud of me. Point: Freddy

I figured that I had won, but I still didn't know what Tommy had done yet.

While we were closing the bar, I was extra cautious of Tommy's whereabouts and actions. I really didn't need to because after he thawed out his keys, he stayed behind the bar cleaning. I was done with my work first and walked out to my car. I said goodbye to Tommy, and he said goodbye back without skipping a beat. When I found myself about four feet from my car, I stopped to see the 'grand finale'. Tommy first took a roll of plastic wrap from the kitchen and wrapped it around my car about seven or eight times so the doors wouldn't open. Then, he stuck pats of butter underneath all of the door handles. Finally, he shoved limes in my tailpipes.

These were all very good moves, but there were flaws. The plastic wrap was way too easy to see, so I figured that couldn't have been all. The butter had melted and ran down the sides of my car. It's Arizona; heat does these things…in January. There still had to be more I thought. I saw *48 Hours*; I knew what he did. I then went back to find the limes in the tailpipes.

As I tried removing all of the items from my car, Jake Guzman stuck his head out the door by my car.

"Freddy, are you doing okay? I mean, is your car running okay?" He said this with a shit-eating grin on his face.

"I'm sure it will run fine after I get the limes out of the tailpipes!" I said back.

I found out later that Tommy was standing right next to Jake the whole time waiting for me to start my car. I bet he was waiting for the backfiring to signal his triumph like fireworks on the Forth Of July. Tommy was pretty upset after I still found the limes after everything else.

What The Hell Is Wrong With You!?

Tommy and I never had another war like that again, which is probably a good thing. One of us would probably loose an eye. However the next day, I did put butter on his door handles. I never heard anything about that, oh well.

What do you think? Who won the battle? Voice your opinion at www.whatthehelliswrongwithyou.com! I think I won, but I'm a little bias.

What The Hell Is Wrong With You!?

Chapter Treintitres: What? You're Done Already!?

Whew. I never thought I would make it to the conclusion. I've impressed myself. I hope you got something out of this book. If anything, you got a tip chart, a glossary of common restaurant words, the 'levels of drunkenness' idea, and you learned to count to 33 in Spanish! There's something!

I'm going to try to sum up the book in this last chapter for those of you who start books from the wrong cover. I know that just about everyone reading this probably has worked or currently works in the hospitality industry and are not one of my stereotypical 'idiots'. Please don't take any offence to the first-to-third-person stories. I wrote the book like I was talking to you from the next bar stool over.

I do hope that you found an abundance of humor in the stories I've told. That was the whole point of taking the book this far. I also encourage you to (legally) share this with others. One of my friends shared an idea with me: they want to buy an extra copy for *that one friend* that does the embarrassing faux pas described herein. I'm not trying to hurt anyone's feelings and if I did hurt your feelings, well, life's a bitch, sorry.

If you are one of the idiots, I do pray that this has shown you some light and gave you reason to change your ways for the better. Don't worry, one day we will all get along together just fine. I can't see bartenders and grouchy, ignorant customers gathered around a campfire singing *Kumbayah* any time soon, but there should always be hope.

If you liked this book and would like to submit feedback, you can go to www.whatthehelliswrongwithyou.com. If you didn't like this book, then how the hell did you make it all the way to the end?

What The Hell Is Wrong With You!?

Just so you know, there is a sequel to this. More things have happened and will happen. I've met newer idiots with newer, more thought provoking, illogical nuances. It will be called *What The Hell Is Wrong With You...Now!?* It will be available on the website as soon as possible.

I would now like to finish off with some vital points about life, death, and the service industry.

✓ Always tip employees that should be tipped. Servers, bartenders, tattoo artists, taxi drivers, concierges, and anyone else who has to clean up after your filthy ass. Remember; it's not only expected by us as our primary income – but by the restaurant and the IRS. This is how all restaurant people think: if you don't have the money to tip, don't go out. Go the store and buy your drinks there. There is no nice way to put that.

✓ Please be responsible when you go out drinking. There are only a few exceptions to drinking yourself into oblivion. And no, it's not 'any day that ends in –y'. Holidays like St. Patrick's Day, New Years Eve, Cinco de Mayo, Thanksgiving, and your birthday. Those days, through the ages, have been designated for that purpose (based on society, not tradition). I don't think anyone should binge on Christmas, Easter, Kwanzaa, Chanukah, Yom Kipper or any other religious holiday. Call it a warning.

WHAT THE HELL IS WRONG WITH YOU!?

✓ Remember that alcohol works by cutting off the oxygen to your brain. Anything carbonated and/or sugary will add to this effect (mind eraser anyone?). Your brain may still need a little oxygen later on that night, so do be careful.

✓ **DON'T DRINK AND DRIVE!!** I know that I have done it myself, and every time that I have, it's been very stupid. Not only could a DUI change your life for a very long time, but you could kill someone and change many lives forever. Unfortunately, we all have heard stories about drunk drivers' accidents. Always remember, and I will do the same, there's nothing un-cool about taking a cab home. We'll call this our little pact. God and I know how many people could read this. Okay, that was the public service announcement.

✓ Always remember to treat each other in the same way you would want to be treated. The world would be a better place if we all did that one simple thing. When you are at a bar or a restaurant and you think your server or bartender is rude, or snotty, or cocky; remember that it could just be a reflection of yourself.

✓ No matter how angry you get at a rude and inconsiderate customer in the hospitality industry, don't spit or pee in people's food or drink – it's just wrong.

✓ Most importantly – don't be such a bitch!

WHAT THE HELL IS WRONG WITH YOU!?

'Have a nice day! Thanks for stopping by! Hope to see you again real soon! Bye-bye now!'

WHAT THE HELL IS WRONG WITH YOU!?

GLOSSARY OF TERMS

 # - Top- (top) *n,* a name identifying when a server acquires a new table; the number amount equals the amount of people (e.g. four-top, two-top, etc.)

10 Percenter- (ten per cent' er) *n,* a person who only leaves ten percent of his or her total bill, usually found in droves

12 Step Program- (twelv' step prô'gram) *n,* a system based on a program of recovery from addiction providing 12 progressive steps toward attainment

12 Steps of Service- (twelv' steps uv sûr'vis) *n,* a system of giving service providing 12 progressive steps towards attainment (coincidence or irony?)

3 Compartment Sinks- (thrê kem pärt'ment singk) *n,* the sink system found behind a bar with three areas of cleaning; soap, rinse, and sanitize.

5 Second Rule- (fïv si kond' rool) *n* ,the amount of time a consumable can remain on the floor and still be used, practiced primarily in unsanitary conditions

86- (â'tê síks) *v.t.,adj,.-ed* **1.** to refuse service to a customer and deny access forever **2.** used to denote a certain product that has depleted until more is ordered

After-hours Party- (af'ter ou'ers pär'tê) *n,* a social gathering after normal business or legal hours

All Day- (ôl dâ) *adj,* denoting a total of one particular item needed at one time

Apron (Don't tug)- (â'pren) *n,* a piece of material worn around the pants with pockets to hold paper, books, money, etc.; not to be used as a device to hold the attention of the wearer by pulling on it

What The Hell Is Wrong With You!?

Ass Kisser- (as kis'er) *n,* a person who uses praise towards a manager/customer to find personal advancement or money sometimes at the expense of coworkers' tolerances

Autograt- (ô'tô grät) *v,* to add a server's gratuity onto a check's total to thwart the actions of a **cheap ass**

Bar Time- (bär tîm) *n,* the time used in many bars that is actually fifteen to twenty minutes ahead of the actual time; usually used for the employees to close early

Bar Trick- (bär trik) *n,* a clever or ingenious device or maneuver used for entertainment and sometimes to gain money on doubt of ability; usually based on a brainteaser

Behind You- (bi hînd' yoo) *idiom,* phrase used to alert someone of your presence out of his or her field of vision; also see **sexual harassment**

Bev-nap- (bev nap) *n,* a square piece of paper usually 4" by 4" used as a landing pad for a drink; also used in **bar tricks**

Bitters- (bit'erz) *n,* drink flavoring with bitter herbs used in mixed drinks; (mixed with soda water) used to offset a **hangover** or cure hiccups

Bleach and Ammonia- (blêch and e môn'yä) *n,* mixture some idiots use for cleaning; teargas

Blow- (blô) *v,***1.** what a keg does when it reaches empty **2.** (followed by a pronoun) derogatory term of endearment **3.** proposition of action; see **sexual harassment**

Bombed- (bomd) *adj,***1.** intoxicated, high **2.** instantly busy in a restaurant or bar; see **rush**

Break The Seal- (brâk tha sêl) *v, idiom,* to urinate for the first time in one night of drinking usually causing the urge to urinate frequently

Burn Ice- (bûrn ïs) *v,* to run hot water into an ice bin to remove the ice, necessary in finding broken glass in ice

What The Hell Is Wrong With You!?

Burnt Out- (bûrnt out) *adj,* used to describe a person with fatigue, frustration, or apathy resulting from too much work and stress; me

Bustub or Busstub- (bus'tub) *n,* a container with the approximate measurements of 2'x3'x½'; used primarily for the storage and transportation of used dishes

Campers- (kam'perz) *pl n,* people that will sit at a table after the function of visiting a restaurant is completed; people that take up server's real estate hindering their money making ability

CC- (sê sê) *n, abrv.,* used to denote credit card, cottage cheese, cheese crisp, crappy customer, the guitarist of *Poison,* or Canadian Club™; dependent on context

Cocktail- (kok'tâl) *n, v,* **1.** a drink containing alcohol **2.** to wait on tables near a bar; service usually restricted to drinks

Crew or Team- (kroo; têm) *n,* what restaurant employees should be together to work effectively; usually a fallacy

Cut Off- (kut'ôf') *v, adj,* **1.** to refuse further drink service to an obviously intoxicated patron **2.** description of a person that can not receive any more alcohol

Cut The Floor- (kut tha flôr) *idiom, v,* **1.** a request to let a server leave for the day resulting in larger **stations 2.** when a manager reduces the amount of employees working in the restaurant

Dead- (dêd) *adj,* used to describe a situation in a restaurant or bar with few to no customers

Dead-groggy- (dêd'grog'ê) *adj,* dazed and weakened sensation brought on in a **dead** situation; not recoverable and usually shows it's effect in a late **rush**

Decaf- (dë'kaf') *n,* name of coffee or tea that does not contain caffeine; what customers receive when there is no regular coffee left (it's happened to you too!)

WHAT THE HELL IS WRONG WITH YOU!?

Disco- (dis'kô) *abrev,* short for discount (e.g. senior disco); not to be confused with people dancing

Dragging- (drag'ing) *v,* **1.** to be tired, not moving fast **2.** to be missing items of a completed order from a kitchen or a bar

Drink Mat- (dringk mat) *n,* small brown rubber pad with a hollow cavity and support to rest glasses on, where drinks are usually made/mixed; see **mat shot**

Drink Rail- (dringk räl) *n,* the recessed area on the bar that separates the bartender and the surface of the bar; used to catch a drink that has been knocked over

Drop- (drop) *v,* **1.** to prepare (food) by either setting it down on a cooking surface or into a cooking medium **2.** what I do with products almost every time I use a tray

Dying Food- (dî'ing food) *n,* food that has been waiting for a long time to be received; food that is becoming cold, inedible, or not servable

Eating On The Line- (ët'ing on tha lîn) *v,* in violation of **health code**; eating food around or off of a food preparation area; usually done by employees that get yelled at by managers, or done by managers without repercussion

Emergency Exit- (I mûr'jen sê eg'sit) *n,* a marked door with a very loud alarm on the handle to denote an emergency; a name given to the triggered alarm when activated by mistake about 12 times a month

Expo- (ek'spô) *n,* the person that offers communication between the kitchen and the servers, responsible for the organization of product in high volume situations; someone to blame when an order is messed up; see **fib**

Fib - (fib) *n, v,* a mistruth, small or trivial lie; (in restaurant business) to use a scapegoat to avoid receiving blame from a customer, usually a cook, **expo,** or **FNG**

What The Hell Is Wrong With You!?

Flag Down- (flag doun) *v,* a usually unnecessary and/or obnoxious gesture from a customer to get the attention of a server or bartender

Flash Blend- (flash blend) *v,* to add effervesce to an un-carbonated beverage by putting the ingredients in a blender for just under a second

Floatie (Bug)- (flo'të) *n,* an unknown substance found in or on the surface of a drink

Flustered-(flus'terd) *adj,* being overwhelmed by numerous things in a **mental list**, not being able to think straight or remain organized; also see **weeded**

Food Cost- (food'kôst) *n,* a controllable expense affected by food that is wasted, made numerous times (due to **expo**), or food eaten by management and/or employees

Free-Pour- (frë poor) *v,* to pour liquor through a spout without the use of a **jigger**. Measured by counting to four to approximate a 1¼-ounce shot

Frozen- (fröt'sen) *adj,* a drink that has been blended with ice in a blender; usually found in frou-frou drinks or ones with little potency

Fruit Tray- (froot'trä) *n,* a box usually located in the **service well** containing olives, cherries, and other fruits used for decoration on drinks

FNG- ('ef en jê) *n, abrev,* Fucking New Guy; term given to a new employee that usually makes a lot of mistakes

George- (jôrj) *n,* a good tipper; an exclamation to express astonishment and/or approval

Ginger Ale- (jin'jer äl) *n,* carbonated soft drink made with an extract of ginger; in most cases in restaurants that do not carry it, Sprite with a splash of Coke (surprise!)

What The Hell Is Wrong With You!?

Graveyard- (grâv'yärd) *adj,* to denote a shift that will last throughout the night, overnight shift

Guest Check Average (GCA)- (gest chek av'er ij) *n,* the average amount of all checks for a server or bartender in a shift; usually increased by suggestive selling and high-ticket items

Hangover- (hang'ö'ver) *n,* the disagreeable aftereffects of alcohol; what many people in the bar business suffer on a regular basis

Happy Birthday- (hap'ë bûrth'dâ') *n,* a customary song sung to celebrate one's calendar day of birth; a song that some restaurants force their employees to humiliate themselves with; see **self-respect**

Health Code- (helth köd) *n,* laws that assure sanitation in a bar or restaurant, enforced and broken by employees and managers alike

'Hook it up'- (hök et up) *n,* **1.** a phrase used by a poor tipper in a restaurant or bar to persuade the server or bartender to dispense more alcohol or food for little or no cost **2.** an untrue gesture used to suggest there will be a large tip received by someone for some service; a fallacy

Hot- (hot) *adj,* denoting something with a high temperature; usually something not believed by an informed customer until that customer burns themselves; an attractive person, see **hottie**

Hottie (Stops Progress)- (hot'ë) *n,* a person that is sexy or attractive enough to stop the progress of a bar or restaurant; the only accepted attribute to a reduction of productivity

Ice Scoop- (îs scoop) *n,* a hand held shovel shaped tool to put ice in a glass or blender; what is usually buried under the ice when the ice bin is replenished

What The Hell Is Wrong With You!?

Insubordination- (in'se bôr'dn'a'shen) *n,* to not do what is told by a manager; what I usually get in trouble for; see **happy birthday**

Jigger- (jig'er) *n,* a tool found behind the bar used to measure 1¼ ounces of liquor or one legal shot of alcohol in the state of Arizona

Language Barrier- (lang'gwij bar'ë ar) *n,* the lack of communication usually between front of house and back of house employees, due to different languages spoken on either side of the **window**; also see **selective hearing**

Liquor Laws- (lik'er lâz) *pl n,* a group of rules that mandate the amounts, times, persons, and areas where alcohol may be served; when broken, fines and jail time for the employees and employers can be enforced

Mad Shitter- (mad shi'tr) *n,* an anonymous person that leaves a mess of excrement in a bathroom; has occurred in numerous places

Mat Shot- (mat shôt) *n,* a drink made out of the contents of a **drink mat**; usually as a disgusting joke on someone

Mental List- (men'tl lîst) *n,* a memorized and constantly changing list of things that need to be done by a restaurant worker, sorted by priority; what can be forgotten with simple distraction

Mom-Server- (mom sûr'ver) *n,* a veteran server in a restaurant that does not change anything, regardless of **policy**; a person that would rather ostracize a stupid **FNG** than help one

Monkey Dish- (mung'kë dîsh) *n,* a small bowl with a diameter of about 4 inches; used for side items, usually liquid

Murphy's Law- (mûr'feez lâ) *n,* if there is a chance for something to go wrong, it will; applies in tenfold in the restaurant business

WHAT THE HELL IS WRONG WITH YOU!?

One-timer- (wun tï'mr) *n,* a person that will send his or her server or bartender on a trips to retrieve things that they need one item at a time; a person that doesn't ask for five things at once, rather one different thing five times

One-timing- (wun tï'm'ing) *v,* the act of sending someone on numerous tasks without consolidation; what people do to waste the time of restaurant workers

Over/Understaffed- (ö'ver un'der staft) *n,* a situation occurring from mistakes made on either a schedule or over exaggeration or lack of observation of a local event or promo that effects customer flow in a restaurant

Paper Cost- (pâ'per kôst) *n,* a controllable expense affected by paper products including to go boxes/cups and napkins

Party- (pär'tê) *n,* a person or group of people denoted by number that visit a restaurant (e.g. party of twenty)

Patio Heaters- (pä'tê ô' hê'trz) *pl n,* the strange, metal, palm tree shaped things found on an outdoor patio that emanate heat

Peanut Rail- (pê'nut' räl) *n,* the outside edge of many bars where the cross section would have the shape of a peanut; what you lean on when you sit at a bar

Permagrin- (per'mâ'grin) *n,* a smile maintained by a hospitality industry worker regardless of the actual feelings possessed by said hospitality industry worker

Plastic- (plas'tik) *adj,* to go items; what products are placed in to avoid having to clean and reuse them; how laziness attributes to **paper cost**

Policy- (pol'e sê) *n,* rules set forth by a company showing how it wants it's employees to act to promote profit and efficiency; what gets broken on a day-to-day basis; something that, without damaging repercussions, should be broken in the interest of customer service

What The Hell Is Wrong With You!?

Power Trip- (pou'er trîp) *n,* an abuse of power, demanding others to do things for no apparent reason, doing wrong without accepting, admitting, or fixing what they have done; what happens to most newly appointed managers and/or head servers

Rezi- (rezi) *abrv,* reservation; a called in request to be served at a certain time; a good way to affect a server(s) income by not showing up

Rocks- (röx) *pl n,* a slang term used to describe ice cubes in a drink usually containing alcohol

Roll Silver- (rôl sil'ver) *idiom, v,* the tedious act of rolling a spoon, knife, and fork into a napkin for easier distribution; also see **sidework**

Round- (røwnd) **1.** *adj,* A rudimentary shape used to denote circular, not to be confused with 'square' (see pg. 53) **2.** *n,* A word to denote one's desire to acquire a new beverage for **every person in the party**.

Rush- (rush) *n,* a period of time when a restaurant or bar gets very busy, usually at any given moment with little or no warning

Sanitary- (san'i ter'ê) *adj,* to be clean enough not to promote disease, sickness, bacteria, mold, and/or fungus; should be used in action and cleanliness

Sat- (sat) *adj,* when a restaurant employee acquires a new table; *idiom-*'you just got sat'

Screwed- (skrood) *adj,* when you realize you just got the short end of the stick, the raw end of the deal, the bad side, etc.; getting trapped into the restaurant industry; also when you receive a bad tip

Section- (sek'shen) *n,* an area containing tables that one server is assigned to; also known as the floor or a **station**

WHAT THE HELL IS WRONG WITH YOU!?

Selective Hearing- (si lek'tiv hêr'ing) *n,v,* **1.** ignorance from a bartender or server that pretends not to hear you regardless of how much you yell, whistle and clap **2.** When a person from a different origin than the speaker knows the speaker's language, but pretends not to as to avoid added work **3.** when a child or animal ignores a parent or master

Self-Respect- (self rë'spekt) *n,* consideration of one's dignity or one's character; usually lost when you have to do silly shit like sing **happy birthday**, or be an **ass-kisser**

Service Bar- (sûr'vis bär) *n,* a small bar usually hidden in the back that makes drinks for the servers in some restaurant during high volume situations; where a bartender works on the **tip-out** from servers

Service Well- (sûr'vis wel) *n,* an area of a bar where the server(s) get drinks for (their) tables; an area where customers should not order, and certainly should not stand

Sexual Harassment- (sek'shoo el he ras'ment) *n,* lewd or obscene jokes, remarks, or gestures that happen on a day to day, almost minute to minute basis; used as a basis of law suits when someone either takes the harassment too far, or someone can't take a joke

Sidework- (sîd'werk) *n,* extra duties that every restaurant worker needs to do nearing the end of a shift; usually including tasks of cleaning, restocking, and to **roll silver**

Slammed- (slamd) *v,* to be caught in a **rush**; to get instantly busy

Smell Test- (smel test) *n,* a test done by many bartenders and/or cooks to assure the freshness of perishable item before their use using the smell of the said product

Smoke Breaks- (smôk bräk) *n,* any opportunity for a restaurant worker to go outside, or in back, to smoke a cigarette; a necessity to regular smokers in the restaurant industry to cope with the stress

What The Hell Is Wrong With You!?

Soda Box- (sö'da böks) *n,* the box that contains syrup for the soda systems; when empty, the machine tries to equalize the pressure and makes an audible, repetitive, and annoying 'pish' sound

Soda Gun- (sö'da gun) *n,* the hand held device that is used to dispense soda and water for drinks; it can also be used as an effective never-ending water pistol by putting a finger over the end of the nozzle

Soda Machine/Fountain- (sö'da me shen' foun'tn) *n,* a fixed machine used to dispense soda that the servers use; the same machines found at convenience stores

Spanglish- (spang'glîsh) *n,* a unique language derived from mostly English and some Spanish; usually characterized by a normal sentence containing normal English words followed by an -o (e.g. 'I need-o you-o to make-o more food-o!')

Speed Opener- (spëd ô'pe ner) *n,* a long, flat piece of metal with a hole at each end used to pry off bottle caps from beer bottles in one fast motion (see front cover, there is one in my right hand)

Speed Rail- (spëd räl) *n,* a stainless steel shelf located on the bartender's side of the bar at knee level that holds the bottles of liquor; usually lined with a thin rubber (mat) netting

Split Checks- (split cheks) *pl n,* numerous checks created from one larger check; usually not an easy task to do especially with large **parties** that shouldn't need every person separated further wasting restaurant workers time

Stab- (stab) *v,* **1.** to puncture or penetrate; see **sexual harassment** **2.** to put a ticket on an upright nail (spindle) to keep it for future reference if needed

Station- (stä shen) *n,* **1.** an area of product preparation denoted by the product (e.g. soda station) **2.** see **section**

Stiffed- (stift) *adj,* to not receive a tip from a **tight wad** or **cheap ass** further hindering a server or bartender's personal income

Stopper Pour- (stä per poor) *n,* a special spout containing ball bearings that use air displacement to measure out 1¼-ounces of alcohol – usually malfunctions stopping too early.

Store and Pour- (stôr'n'pôr) *n,* a refillable plastic bottle used to store and dispense fruit juices and drink mixes; usually the container used in the **smell test**

Sugared Rim-(shoog'erd rîm) *n,* a glass with sugar on the rim for frou-frou drinks; usually a time consuming task preparing a sugared rim glass that takes away service from all other patrons

Swipee/Mag Card/Key Card- (swî'pee) *n,* a card used to access computer systems in most bars and restaurants; in some restaurants, a mandatory thing to have

Tab- (täb) *n,* A running total of one's current debt to a bar or restaurant. *Syn-* bill, check, ticket, total, invoice, itemized account *Origin-* informal – short for TABULATION

Table Hog- (tä'bel hôg) *n,* a person that takes more tables than any other server; one who purposely seats him or herself tables in his or her station until it's full

Table Tents- (tä'bel tents) *pl n,* promotional devices found on tables and in **drink rails** to advertise specials and products in a bar or restaurant

Tight Wad or Cheap Ass-(tît wad)(chëp as) *n,* a person that does not tip well due to the fact that they would rather save a buck than do what is right and avoid upsetting someone by decreasing their primary income

WHAT THE HELL IS WRONG WITH YOU!?

Tip- (tip) *n,v,* **1.** gratuity **2.** to give a gratuity **3.** a customary accepted and expected tradition in bars and restaurants across the country; the primary compensation for a worker in said industry

Tip Chart- (tip chärt) *n,* a mathematical table showing what to properly tip; primarily based on a 15%, 18% or 20% structure (see pg 121)

Tip-Out- (tip'out) *n,* an amount of money that is given to one tipped employee to another employee that had helped them throughout the shift (e.g. service bartender, **expo,** busser)

Tolerance- (tol'er ens) *n,***1.** the level of endurance one has while drinking; holding liquor **2.** the ability to remain smiling in the face of lost wages, humiliation, and/or stress; see **permagrin**

Trailer Tips- (trâ'ler tips) *n,* **tips** that are substandard, bad tips; usually found in succession in a given shift

Tray Jack- (trâ jak) *n,* a foldable leg network that is used to act as a temporary table for large trays in a restaurant; system resembles 'TV trays'

Turn 'n Burn- (tûrn'n'bûrn) *v,* the act of getting people to sit down, eat, and pay in an expedient manner to use that one table as many times as possible in a given **rush**

Twist- (twist) *n,* **1.** a (usual) lemon rind run around the rim of a cocktail and then left in the drink as garnish to give the hint of lemon **2.** a dance made popular by Chubby Checker **3.** what the bartender does to my arm when he or she asks me if I would like another drink

Walk In- (wôk în) *n,* a large refrigeration unit used to store perishable items in bars and restaurants; noted for it's ability for one or more person(s) to actually be in (see **sexual harassment**)

What The Hell Is Wrong With You!?

Water Drinkers- (wô'ter dring'krs) *pl n,* people that will sit at a table in a restaurant and/or bar and order only water to drink, on occasion these people will make their own lemonade with available sugar and lemons; usually indicated by not leaving a good **tip** (due to percentage of low guest check); regardless of how many hundreds of refills they may need

Weeded- (wê'dîd) *adj,* when someone has too many things in a restaurant or bar to handle alone, having an overloaded **mental list**; also see **slammed, bombed**

Wet Floor Sign- (wet flôr sîn) *n,* a notice primarily designed to alert one of a floor with a slippery footing due to liquid; now used solely as a legal disclaimer so when one falls, one cannot sue

Wheel- (hwêl) *n,* a system used to keep incoming orders to a kitchen or bartender in order and laid out for better viewing; *orig*-an actual horizontally mounted wheel with sectioned off, spring loaded holders for hand written tickets in the land before technology

Window- (win'doe) *n,* a large hole in the wall that divides the kitchen to the rest of the restaurant or bar, usually heated by powerful heat lamps; used to hold prepared food until the server, bartender, manager, or **expo** can deliver it

Write Up- (rît'up) *n,* a document used to record a mishap or blunder and what disciplinary action taken to correct it; usually used numerous times as an empty threat, or only once as a device of termination

WHAT THE HELL IS WRONG WITH YOU!?

YOU WANT MORE!?

If any of you out there would like more copies of this book, there are a few ways to accomplish this.

1. Go to www.whatthehelliswrongwithyou.com and purchase online.
2. Mail in the order form below to the address that it says
3. Go to local promotions in Tempe, Arizona (on the website)
4. Find out which retail outlets supply copies (also on the website)

I'LL GIVE YOU MORE!

What The Hell Is Wrong With You!?

Qty-_____x $12.95-$_____
Add $2 for shipping and handling-$_____
Add $2 for Priority Mail delivery-$_____
Total- $_____

Please allow 14 days for normal delivery

Name: _____

Address: _____

City: _____State: _____ Zip: _____

Email Address: _____

Send this form (or a copy) and check or money order for the total above to:

Tempe Thunder Press
P.O. Box 1791
Tempe, Arizona 85280-1791

Thank you for your order!!